WHAT YOUR STOCKBROKER DOESN'T WANT YOU TO KNOW

By Bruce Sankin

Copyright 1990, 1992 by Bruce Sankin.
Revised 1992, 2002
Published by: Bruce N. Sankin & Associates,
PO Box 77-1502, Coral Springs, Florida 33077
Library of Congress Catalog
Card number: 90-86108
ISBN: 0962981117

TABLE OF CONTENTS

About the Author

Bruce Sankin is a former stockbroker, having worked for Prudential-Bache & Dean Witter. He has a Bachelor of Science degree in finance and was a member of the Law Society.

Mr. Sankin writes a column on arbitration and has been interviewed in many publications like Money Magazine and The Wall Street Journal. He has appeared on national television and has been used for his expert opinion in arbitration cases. He is also an arbitrator and mediator specializing in securities.

He currently is an investment counselor based in Coral Springs, Florida. In addition to writing for professional journals and researching for high quality investments, Mr. Sankin also advises individuals, pension plans, and corporations on mutual funds, CD s, bonds, and money market investments.

If you lost money on specific investments that you feel were unjustified, contact me and I will review your situation.

Mr. Sankin also uses his expert knowledge in arbitration and mediation in the securities industry to advise his clients on the strengths and weaknesses of their claim and the potential monetary value of their arbitration case.

If you lost money on specific investments that you feel were unjustified, contact me and I will review your situation.

For more information, or if you have any comments about your own investment experiences that would be helpful to other investors, or if you would like to comment about the book, please write:

Bruce Sankin
PO Box 77-1502
Coral Springs, Florida 33077
954 346-8585
bsankin@yahoo.com
www.investorsrights.com

As seen on the Internet

"CAN YOU GET BACK INVESTMENT LOSSES?"

I've been a securities arbitrator since 1992 and mediator for the NASD since 1996. During this period of time I have been involved as a neutral in the successful resolution of many cases. In 1991 I authored the book "WHAT YOUR STOCKBRO-KER DOESN'T WANT YOU TO KNOW" which told people how the arbitration process works and how to get money back from brokerage firms. Having over 15 years of professional experience in the securities industry I know how firms think in evaluation the value of a client's complaint. After reviewing the facts of a complaint, I can give you a neutral objective evaluation of what a firm might pay a client in a mediation to eliminate the uncertainty of going to an arbitration. My expert neutral advise will give you the options before you go to the expense of hiring an attor-ney and giving them a retainer of a few thousand $$. I will give you an unbiased evaluation of your strengths and weaknesses in order for you to determine the probable monetary outcome of your dispute. When you call I will give you refer-ences at the NASD and I will fax you my Mediator Disclosure Report (This is sent out by the NASD to prospective brokerage firms and claimants who would want to use my services). I will review the information you give me during our conver-sation. It is possible you will have to send me statements and documents for me to give a more detailed opinion.

Bruce Sankin
PO Box 77-1502
Coral Springs, Florida 33077
(954) 346-8585
bsankin@yahoo.com
www.investorsrights.com

SPECIAL BONUS

Free Telephone Consultation
with the Author

PLUS

$100 Credit Towards
Your Case Evaluation!

Bruce Sankin
PO Box 77-1502
Coral Springs, Florida 33077
(954) 346-8585
bsankin@yahoo.com
www.investorsrights.com

PREFACE

This publication is designed to provide accurate and authoritative information in regard to the subject matter covered. Neither the author nor the publisher is engaged in rendering legal, accounting, or other professional service by means of this book. If legal advice or other expert assistance is required, the services of a competent professional should be sought.

Brokerage houses like Prudential Bache, Merrill Lynch, Paine Webber, and others provide a valuable service to individuals and corporations; they offer their clients different investment choices for their money. Each firm has its own policies. However, the similarities between the major brokerage houses make these examples generally applicable to all brokers.

In general stockbrokers, except for very rare exceptions, deal honestly and with integrity with their clients. But you should always understand that they are in business to make money.

If you do business at Merrill Lunch, Dean witter, Prudential Bache, Shearson Lehman Hutton, Paine Webber, or other full service brokerage firms, the person you deal with may be called an account executive, assistant vice-president, first vice-president, certified financial planner, financial advisor, or investment planner. Whatever that person s title, if he does not make a salary, but only makes and income on what he buys or sells in stocks and bonds, insurance, mutual funds, direct investments, etc., he is a **COMMISSIONED SALESMAN**. To make a living, he must generate commissions. He is there to convince you to buy or sell something to generate a trade. By knowing this, this book will help you get the best value for your money when you deal with commissioned salesmen because, usually, **ALL COMMISSIONED SALESMEN ARE WILLING TO NEGOTIATE.**

This book will show you ways to receive investment advice without the bias that can be inherent in the commission brokerage houses, or help you to be aware of the bias.

This book will also show you what remedies you may have against your broker or brokerage house, based on their advice to you, and how you may fate in an arbitration proceeding.

This book is dedicated to showing you how to give you stockbroker less of your money so you can keep more of it.

Update 2002

Since the last revision of this book in 1992 the brokerage industry has changed dramatically. There are more discount houses and now online trading which didn't exist in 1992. There have been many consolidations in the major wire houses. Competition has grown for your money. When I wrote in 1990 and said "all commissioned salesmen are willing to negotiate" it is more true today then ever before. Also if you lost money there is additional ways to get part or all of your money back from the brokerage firms.

CHAPTER 1

HOW TO SAVE MONEY
ON BUYING AND SELLING STOCKS

A stockbroker receives a commission for the service of buying or selling your stock. If you want to know your commission cost before deciding to make a trade, just call your stockbroker and he will be able to give it to you. It should be noted that your broker has the authority to offer you a 5%-20% discount. However, most brokers will not volunteer this information, since it means that they will make less money from the trade. Therefore, if you want the discount you must ask your stockbroker for it.

It is not in the stockbroker s best interest to give you a large discount because some brokerage firms pay less of a commission to the broker if the discount exceeds a certain percentage. Stockbrokers work on what is called a grid. The percentage of commission a stockbroker receives is dependent upon the amount of business the broker generates for the brokerage firm. For example, if the stockbroker is on a 35% payout grid, he is entitled to 35% of the commission that the brokerage firm charges you. If, however, the broker discounts a stock trade more than his firm permits, they may pay him less than 35% of the commissions.

Remember what your stockbroker does not want you to know, **BROKERAGE FIRMS WILL ALLOW LARGER DISCOUNTS.** Sometimes the broker will need his office manager s approval. Ask your broker to ask his manager for a larger discount. Many managers may not want you to know that the firm can offer a larger discount because managers receive a percentage of the total revenue the office generates, so larger discounts will mean less money for him.

If you want to buy 200 shares of stock at a price of $20.00 per share, the total cost would be $4,000.00 plus your stockbroker s commission. At a full service brokerage firm, the commission rate quoted by a stockbroker could be as much as 3.1% of the purchase price of the stock, or $125, in the above example. This is very expensive. Usually a fair price is considered to be between 1% and 2%. Thus, you can, and should, negotiate with your broker.

An alternative to negotiating with your broker over his commission is to tell your broker that you want to trade on a per share basis. Trading on a per share basis is when you pay a commission on each share of stock that you purchase as opposed to a percentage of the total purchase price of that stock, i.e. a commission. It is possible to negotiate a $.10 to $.25 per share cost with your broker. **Tell your broker what you are willing to pay him.** If your stockbroker tells you he will not do the trade at the commission cost you want, then find a broker who will. There will always be stockbrokers who are looking for business.

If you are directing the transactions in your account, i.e. telling your broker what to buy or sell, then his services are of limited value to you anyway since he is merely an order taker. Thus, you should have a say in deciding how much money his services are worth.

You must not forget that a stockbroker is a commissioned salesman, he wants and needs your business. Do not believe your broker if he says that he does not. **That is how he makes his living.** He does not want to lose your business or for you to get advice from anyone else. And, if your broker really does not want to do your trade at your price, do not worry, you will always find one who will, you just need to look.

CHAPTER 2

BONDS

If you ask, your stockbroker has to tell you his commission on a purchase or sale of a stock. Likewise, if you ask, he has to tell you the sales charge when you purchase or sell a mutual fund. However, when you want to buy a bond, whether it is a tax free municipal bond, most corporate bonds, or a treasury bond, your broker does not have to tell what he and the firm are making on the transaction. This is because bonds are bought and sold on a mark-up or mark-down basis and mark-ups or mark-downs do not have to be disclosed. Buying or selling a bond with a mark-up and mark-downs rather than commissions is called buying or selling net .

If you go to your broker to buy a tax free municipal bond and he says the price is $10,000.00 net, he will generally tell you that the price includes commissions. You can however still find out what the cost to you of the transaction is by asking the broker what the firm would pay you if you wanted to sell the same bond to them. If, for example, the answer was that the firm would pay you $9,600.00 if they were buying it from you, then the actual cost (spread) of the bond is $400.00 or 4%.

If you ask your broker what the buying or selling price of a bond is, he usually has to call or wire his bond department to get the information. He then puts his own mark-up on top of that. Receiving information from the bond department usually takes from 15 minutes to an hour. (If your broker can give you the information right away, be skeptical unless this information is on his computer because individual brokers do not have discretion to set the price at which a firm will buy or sell a bond). The difference between the bid and ask (sell and buy) given to the broker by the bond department is generally 1/4 to 1% spread. This spread is what the bond department makes on the bond. Then the stockbroker adds on his commission which will usually be between 1/2% and 4%. **What you, as the client, are probably unaware of is that the broker has substantial freedom to mark up or mark down the bond depending on what he thinks you will pay for it or sell it for.** On a buy and sell of the same bond, the broker and the brokerage firm together could make as much as 6% on the trade.

What your stockbroker does not want you to know is that you can negotiate bond prices. When he gives you a price for a bond you can usually negotiate between 1/4% and 1% of the price of the bond. On a $25,000.00 purchase or sale, you could save as much as $250.00. If your broker does not want to give you this discount, then call other brokers and tell them what you are looking for. With billions of dollars of bonds for sale everyday, there will be a broker who can usually get your bond at your price. On the other hand, if your broker offers you a bond and, after calling other brokerage firms, you find it to be the best price, quote, and yield — **BUY IT.** Getting what you want is more important then knowing what the brokerage firm makes.

UNIT TRUSTS

In some instances brokerage firms or independent companies put a group of bonds together and sell them as a package. These packages are usually called unit trusts . A unit trust may be preferable to individual bonds because it diversifies the risk among a group of bonds instead of putting all the money into one bond. Another benefit of the unit trust is that interest payments are made monthly as compared to an individual bond, where interests payments are made semi-annually. On the other hand, the cost of buying a unit trust is not cheap; it can range between 4% to 5% and is an integral part of the structure of the trust. Therefore, commissions on unit trusts cannot generally be negotiated.

The purchase of unit trusts is, however, subject to commission discounts in the form of break points . This means that for certain volume purchases the commission will decrease. Common breakpoints in the purchase of unit trusts are $50,000. $100,000. and $250,000.00. Under a $100,000 purchase you may pay 4 3/4 % commission while at $100,000 you may pay 3 1/4%, at $250,000 4% etc. (It should be noted that your broker receives a commission when you buy a unit trust, though not usually when you sell it.)

When you ask about a unit trust, your broker will give you three quotations. He will quote you the price that you will pay if you want to buy it (ask price); the price that you will get if you want to sell it (bid price); and the actual value (par value) of the bonds in each unit of the trust. The par value is also the amount of money you will get back if you hold each unit to maturity (or to the call date, if the unit is priced to call).

When your broker gives you a price and yield on a unit trust make sure he tells you two yields: the current yield and the yield to maturity or to call date. It is also important to find out if the bond in the unit trust has a call feature. This means that the company or municipality can buy the bonds back from the unit trust before maturity. It has no option if the bond gets called. The unit trust must sell it back. Make sure your broker tells you what the yield to call is. It could be a lot less than a yield to maturity or current yield and you do not want any surprises after you buy the unit trust.

Be very careful when your broker gives you a quotation for a current yield on a unit trust that seems higher than an individual bond. If this does occur, ask him for the bid price, the ask price and the par value. For example, if he tells you that you will get 7.75% current return on a unit trust and a comparable individual bond is only giving 7.0% current return, then there is a good chance you are paying a premium for each unit trust.

A premium is the difference between what you pay (ask price) and the actual value (par price). If the ask price for the unit is $1,000.00 per unit and the par price is $900.00 per unit, you are paying $100.00 per unit or 10% more than the actual value. If you bought 10 units at $1,000.00 each and paid $10,000.00 and you held the units to maturity, you would only get back $9,000.00. You would get more income on your units each year, but in the end you would get less principal back then you put in. Premium bonds and unit trusts can be a good investment as long as you understand what you are giving up in principal for the extra yearly income.When buying bonds you should ask your stockbroker about the rating of the bonds or unit trusts. A rating will give you the quality and risk of each bond. The higher the quality, the less the risk, the lower the yield or return on your investment . Conversely, the lower the quality, the higher the risk, the higher the yield. Most bonds are rated by two rating companies: Standard & Poors, commonly know as S&P, and Moody s Investor Service.

The following is Standard & Poor s definition on rating of bonds:

AAA - Debt rated AAA has the highest rating assigned by Standard & Poor s. Capacity to pay interest and repay principal is extremely strong.

AA - Debt rated AA has a very strong capacity to pay interest and repay principal and differs from the higher rated issues only in small degree.

A - Debt rated A has a strong capacity to pay interest and repay principal although it is somewhat more susceptible to the adverse effects of changes in circumstances and economic conditions than debt in higher rated categories.

BBB- Debt rated BBB is regarded as having an adequate capacity to pay inter est and repay principal. Whereas it normally exhibits adequate protection parameters, adverse economic conditions or changing circumstances are more likely to lead to a weakened capacity to pay interest and repay principal for debt in this category than in higher rated categories.

BB, B, CCC, CC, C -
Debt rated BB , B , CCC , CC and C is regarded, on balance, as predominantly speculative with respect to capacity to pay interest and repay principal in accordance with the terms of the obligation. BB indicates the lowest degree of speculation and C the highest degree of speculation. While such debt will likely have some quality and protective characteristics, these are out-weighted by large uncertainties or major risk exposures to adverse conditions.

Bond Investment Quality Standards:
Under present commercial bank regulations issued by the Comptroller of the Currency, bonds rated in the top four categories (AAA , AA , A , BBB , commonly known as Investment Grade ratings) are generally regarded as eligible for bank investment. In addition, the Legal Investment Laws of various states may impose certain rating or other standards for obligations eligible for investment by savings banks, trust companies, insurance companies and fiduciaries generally.

There are also bonds known as nonrated or NR bonds. This means that for some reason S&P and/or Moody s have not rated the quality of that particular bond. It does not mean, however, that there is something wrong with the bond. If you are interested in a nonrated bond, ask your stockbroker to find out the reason why it is not rated. If there is not a good reason why the bond has not been rated, then the best thing to do is to pass on that bond and find another bond with a rating that meets your satisfaction.

Many unit trusts are sold in a secondary market. This means that an individual sold the unit trust before maturity. Often, Unit Trusts sold before maturity are purchased by the brokerage firm and put into the brokerage firm s inventory. This means that you may be able to buy a unit trust that has a higher coupon, (premium) or lower coupon (discount) from the brokerage firms inventory.

Individual bonds and unit trusts have something in common which buyers sometimes are unaware of. The face value of these investments are only paid at maturity. If you sold these investments before maturity, you would get the market value. Market value is the price the brokerage firm is willing to pay. This could be higher or lower than the amount you paid for it. Example: You bought a $10,000 General Electric bond that expires January 1, 1995. If you held the bond to maturity, General Electric would pay you $10,000 on January 1, 1995. If you sold this bond before January 1, 1995, it is strictly the brokerage firm s decision what price they will pay you for the bond.

CHAPTER 3

MUTUAL FUNDS

One of the largest groups of products in the 1980 s, where retail brokers made enormous commissions, was in mutual funds. Mutual funds are a simple way to invest in securities. You tell your stockbroker what you are looking for: stocks; bonds; an aggressive or conservative investment strategy; an income or an appreciation approach; then your broker finds the mutual fund which fits your needs. Since your broker is probably a com-missioned salesman, he will usually attempt to sell you an open ended mutual fund that has a load or sales charge. Some mutual funds have sales charges as high as 8 1/2% (actually 9.3%) of the amount you will invest. That means that if you invest $10,000.00 today, tomorrow your investment will only be worth $9,150.00. Your stockbroker and his firm split the $850.00 differ-ence. If you invest $50,000.00 your sales charge would be $4,250.00. Now we are talking about giving up real money. Most stock funds with front end loads have sales charges between 4% and 8 1/2%. Bond funds have sales charges that range between 3% and 7%. Sales charges are usually reduced the more you invest. This is known as break points or, in simple terms, a volume discount.

In the early 1980 s brokerage firms and mutual fund companies realized people did not like to pay an upfront sales charge, so they invented a new type of sales charge called back-end sales charge , or redemption fees . This means that you may pay a sales charge when you sell your shares back to the fund. Most back-end load mutual funds have an additional annual expense to the shareholder known as the 12b-1 fee. Mutual fund managers say this fee is used to promote and advertise the fund to other potential shareholders. This fee can be as high as 1 1/4% per year. If you hold a mutual fund that has a 12b-1 fee of 1.25% for ten years and then sell it, you will be giving up an additional 12 1/2% of your assets. 12b-1 fees of less than 1/4 of 1% a year really do not make a great difference; however, anything more than that, unless the fund is a stellar performer, is unjustified in my opinion and I would look for another fund.

Stockbrokers do not want you to know that you do not have to buy mutual funds from stockbrokers. If you care about what happens to your money, and are willing to put in a little extra work yourself, you can buy no load mutual funds with the same or similar type of securities and investment objectives your broker would purchase for you with a load. You could possibly save hundreds to thousands of dollars. If you have $50,000.00 to invest, one option would be to call up a stockbroker and set up a meeting. At the meeting you could discuss your financial needs. At the end of the meeting your stockbroker would probably recommend a certain mutual fund. If that mutual fund has a sales charge of 7% you have just paid him $3,500.00 for that one hour of his time. You now have to decide if your face to face meeting with him was worth it. Obviously, a no load fund is preferable to a load fund. And I have not seen any study that has proven that load funds out perform no load funds. In short, a sales charge does not buy superior fund management; all a sales charge buys you is a salesman. Once the money goes into the mutual fund, performance is up to the portfolio manager. Therefore, a no load fund would be more desirable than a load fund since there is no sales charge on a no load fund.

If you took the same hour you spent with the stockbroker and went to the library instead, you could get information on no load funds. One of the best sources is the **Morningstar Mutual Funds Value Report.** This book will give all the information you will ever need to make a fair judgment on over one thousand mutual funds. Many stockbrokers use this book to get the information that they give to their clients. Magazines like

MONEY and **FORBES** publish special editions that describe and rate mutual funds. There are also newsletters that follow the mutual fund industry like **MUTUAL FUND FORECASTER** out of Fort Lauderdale, Florida. This monthly newsletter gives recommendations and updates on most mutual funds. So, with a little effort you can save yourself big money. Your stockbroker does not want you to know that you have alternatives to purchasing load mutual funds.

If you don t want to put in the time and effort to find a no load fund and still want to use the services of a stockbroker to recommend a good family of funds, here is an idea on how to reduce the sales charge. Many excellent family of funds like M.F.S., Putnam, Delaware Group, Kemper, Aim, etc. have different funds within the same family. All of these funds have exchange privileges, which means you can switch from one fund to another at net asset value. What your stockbroker doesn t want you to know is that different funds within the same family have different sales charges. This means you can buy a fund that has a load of 2 1 2% and a week later you can exchange it for a fund you really wanted, which has a 5 3 4% load saving you 3 1 4% on the purchase of the fund. This could be hundreds of dollars or more in savings you don t have to pay your broker. These savings will range from 25%—60% of the sales charge.

There are two types of mutual funds: open-end and closed-end. Open-end mutual funds consist of a portfolio of securities that trade at net asset value, or N.A.V. Net asset value is the total value of the securities in the fund at the end of each trading day divided by the number of shares outstanding of the fund. That is how you get the cost per share of an open-end mutual fund. So, that even if you buy an open-end mutual in the morning, your broker cannot tell you what you paid for the fund until the next day. Open-end also means the number of shares that can be purchased is unlimited. A closed-end fund is a fund which has a limited number of shares.

An open-end fund and a closed-end fund are similar in that they both have securities in their portfolio, they both charge shareholders for expenses, and they both have N.A.V. s; however, unlike shares of a open-end fund, shares of a closed-end fund are traded freely in the open market. This means that shares could be bought and sold either below (a discount) or above (a premium) the fund s net asset value. Since the number of shares of a closed-end fund is limited, the price at which you either buy or sell your shares in the open market will depend on the demand for the shares. Clearly, then, there is an additional risk in a closed-end fund. Not only is there fluctuation in net asset value, but also in the demand for the shares, and because of this, there is also an opportunity. If you purchase shares of a closed-end fund whose shares are selling at a significant discount to the net asset value, it is possible in a rising market that not only will the net asset value increase, but the demand for the shares will also increase. This will narrow the discount and possibly put the share price at a premium to net asset value. You can find specific information on closed-end funds in the **WALL STREET JOURNAL and BARRONS.** They will have the share price, net asset value, and percentage of discount or premium so you can easily be fully informed.

If your broker calls you about a new closed-end fund that is coming to the market, I recommend that you do not purchase it at the initial offering, since the market price is usually at a premium to net asset value. This is due to the fund s initial selling and administrative expenses. As an example, many closed-end funds that came to market in 1988 had an offering price of ten dollars. But the net asset value was $9.30 (usually 7% was expenses). I recommend waiting six months to a year to see how the fund performs, and what the net asset value and demand for the shares are.

One final fact your stockbroker does not want you to know: once the stockbroker purchases the bonds, unit trust, or mutual fund, he has usually already made his commission. Since he cannot make any more commission from these investments, he is usually indifferent about following these investments. Brokers call the money they invested gone , which means they are unable to generate additional commissions from the money. On mutual funds a broker might make a trailer commission from a 12b-1 fee, but this is usually only 10 - 25 basis points per year, very little to give him incentive to follow the performance of the fund. The only way for him to generate additional commissions is for you to sell it and buy something else.

Update 2002

Since most people complained about the high front end commissions, the brokerage firms have created "B and C'" shares. This is where the client buys the funds at Net Asset Value (NAV) but additional expenses or fees known as "12-b1" fees are added annually. This reduces the annual returns of the fund by usually 1%. Brokers still have to get their commission when the fund is sold. The commission in "B" shares is usually 4% of the investment. If you own "B" shares you have to hold the fund for a period of time before you sell it so you don't get charged a redemption fee. Usually six years. With "C" shares, the broker receives 1% at the time of the sale, and 1% annually as long as you hold the fund.

CHAPTER 4

HOW IMPORTANT
IS THE ACCOUNT FORM?

When you go to a brokerage firm to invest your money, you go with the understanding that the information your stockbroker will provide is accurate and truthful, so that you can make an informed decision on your investments.

Usually, the first time you hear about an investment is either in your stockbroker s office or on the phone with your stockbroker. Since he is the professional on investments you accept his advice. You also assume that what he is doing is in your best interest.

A problem can arise months, or sometimes years later when you realize that you were sold an investment that you were unsuited for, or an investment about which you did not understand the risks involved.

If this happens to you, and you and the brokerage firm cannot come to an amicable solution, then arbitration could be your legal remedy.

The arbitration may take place years after the original conversation between you and your stockbroker regarding the investment you purchased.

I can almost guarantee you that the stockbroker will remember the conversation differently than you do, thereby making the verbal discussions unreliable and meaningless. That is why the Account Form, usually the only written document the stockbroker has that describes you, becomes so vital in your defense at arbitration.

Thus, the most important and least understood document the stockbroker has a client fill out is the Client Account Form. Every person must fill out an Account Form to receive an account number. This is mandatory before a transaction between you and your stockbroker can occur.

The Client Account Form might look like a basic questionnaire with simple questions, but it is *the* document that shows if you are suited for certain types of investments. Do not answer these questions lightly or inaccurately. It could cost you dearly in the future.

Before I review the Account Form line by line, I want to emphasize the best advice I can give you. **DON'T EXAGGERATE YOUR EXPERIENCE OR INCOME ON THE ACCOUNT FORM.** If you make $30,000.00 a year do not state anything higher. When the question is about your investment experience in stocks, bonds, commodities, etc., only put the actual number of years you have been an investor. If you are trying to impress the stockbroker, **DON'T!**

Now I will show you how a brokerage firm could interpret your answers on an Account Form. A standard Client Account Form will contain the following questions:

1. **General Information** - name, address, birthdate, social security number, telephone number.
   So far no problem.

2. **Residence** - rent or own. This shows the brokerage firm, right away, that if you own a home, you are not ignorant of all types of investments. Also, if you own a real estate limited partnership you would have some idea of the liquidity and economic risks involved in owning real estate. Thus, if the partnership had decreased in value, you could not claim that you were unaware of the risks in real estate.

3. **Legal residence if different from mailing address** - This shows the brokerage firm if you have more than one home, which is an indication of your assets.

4. **Employment/Job Title/Occupation** - This may show the type of knowledge you might have pertaining to investments in certain industries.

5. **Client state annual income. Client state net worth exclusive of family residence, and estimated liquid net worth. DO NOT EXAGGERATE.** This shows the brokerage

firm what portion of your assets are in a specific investment. Having a diversified portfolio of no more than 2-5% of total assets in one investment may not be worth as much in an arbitration decision as 50% in one investment.

6. **Is the client on a fixed income - Yes or No** - If you are, then say it. By checking this box the stockbroker should be aware that you have no additional income other than your investments, pensions, and/or social security, and that you will probably be a conservative investor.

7. **Is the client an officer, director or 10% stockholder in any corporation** - This tells the brokerage firm that you probably have knowledge about business and investments and also that you have additional assets.

8. **Citizen of U.S.A. (if other please specify).** If you are not a citizen of the U.S., there may be different tax liabilities depending on your investments and the country that you are from. The stockbroker must be aware of this; otherwise, the brokerage firm, not you, could be liable for any losses incurred.

9. **Former client or account with other brokerage firm** This shows the brokerage firm the type of investments that you may have

made in the past. This will also indicate if you are knowledgeable or suited for certain types of investments.

10.   **Investment profile** - Very important! If you want safety of principal and income, **DON'T SAY GROWTH!** Put down only what you want. Also remember, do not put down more investment experience in stock, bonds, options, etc. than what you actually have.

11.   **Introduction** - This is where the brokerage firm finds out how you came to open an account. The options are usually seminars, walk/phone in, advertising, personal acquaintance, and referrals. Seminars, personal acquaintances, and referrals may sound innocent, but let me show you what they imply: If you went to a seminar it shows you go out of your way to get knowledge on specific investments. Brokerage firms may say if you have gone to one seminar you may have gone to many and that you are aware of different types of investments and are probably suited for many investments. If you are referred by a person who is knowledgeable about investments, then there is a good chance you have had discussions about investments, which could imply that you know more about investments than what is stated on

the account form. These are possibilities of how a brokerage firm may look at your account form.

12. **References** - name of bank. If you ever have a problem with the brokerage firm they may want to know about your knowledge of investments. References would be a good place to find out this type of information.

13. **Power of attorney** - This means someone besides yourself has the right to handle the money in your account, as well as decide what investments should be made. Be very careful with this, giving someone else this authority may affect your financial situation forever.

14. **Account description** - cash or margin. Cash accounts are the most common. In a cash account, you buy or sell a security (stock, bond, mutual fund, etc.) and pay or receive 100% of the amount, usually within five business days. A Margin Account gives you the right to borrow money on your account (a loan) by using the securities in the account as collateral.For example: If you buy 100 shares of General Electric at $60.00 a share; the total amount you would owe is $6,000.00. In a Margin Account you could borrow up to 50% of the amount owed, which means you would pay

$3,000.00 and the brokerage firm would lend you the other $3,000.00 for as long as you keep the General Electric stock in your account. Like any other loan, you will pay interest charges to the brokerage firm for as long as you owe them the $3,000.00.

Buying on margin is O.K. **as long as your stockbroker explains, AND YOU UNDER STAND,** both the risks and the benefits. It is very important to update the account form if your situation changes, i.e. a spouse dies, your financial situation changes, you retire, etc. Make sure your stockbroker is notified in writing and a new account form is filled out. In case a dispute arises between you and your broker, another fact that you should know is that the stockbroker must be licensed in the state where you are a permanent resident. If you buy securities from a stockbroker and you lose money, make sure that he was licensed in your state at the time of the transaction. If not, the trade should be voided and you should get all your money back.

CHAPTER 5

WHAT YOU SHOULD KNOW
THAT COULD SAVE YOU MONEY

1.   Tell your broker to send you an old copy of the Standard and Poors (S & P) book. This monthly book gives you the name of issue, ticker symbol, rating, principle business, price range, dividend, yield, price earnings ratio, financial position, capitalization, annual earnings, plus information on over 700 mutual funds every month. Most brokers, after a month or two, throw out their old copies. Most of the information does not change so it is a wealth of information that usually ends up in the waste basket. If you were to pay for a subscription to S & P for a year, you would pay $105.00. So, call your broker and save.
SAVINGS: $105.00

2.   If you are in the market for mutual funds, do a little homework, as I described in Chapter 3, and buy no load funds.
SAVINGS: hundreds to thousands of dollars.

3. If you decide to buy mutual funds or unit trusts from your broker, make sure he tells you about BREAKPOINTS.

    SAVINGS: hundred to thousands of dollars.

4. If you open a margin account at a broker-age firm you should understand what you have at risk. What you are actually doing is taking out a loan and using the securities in your account as collateral. The margin rates charged are usually 1/2% - 2 1/2% over the broker loan rate. **MARGIN RATES CAN USUALLY BE NEGOTIATED.** You can usually negotiate savings of 1/2% - 1% on the rate.

    SAVINGS: If you margin $25,000.00 you could save $125.00 - $250.00 per year.

5. **BEWARE!** There are some mutual funds that charge a sales charge on reinvested income. This means that if you   reinvest your income by buying more shares in the mutual fund, the fund will charge you an additional sales charge to reinvest. So, if you want to reinvest your income, make sure the fund you decide to buy does not have a sales charge to reinvest.

    SAVINGS: percentage of all reinvested income.

6.   If your stockbroker sells you a mutual fund and it **does not perform**, or your investment strategy changes, and your broker tells you to sell the fund and go into another fund, **BEWARE!** Buying a new fund may cost you additional sales charges.   Note, however, that exchanging a fund within the same family of funds may cost you very little.   Another fund within the same family may meet your investment needs, and to exchange from one fund to another, within the same family, usually has no sales charge or a small administrative fee (five to ten dollars). **DON'T SELL IF YOU CAN EXCHANGE.**
SAVINGS: Hundreds to thousands of dollars.

7.   Make sure every question on the account form is answered accurately. Most people do not answer all the questions, and this could be harmful because it is a document that could help you in the future. For example, if you state on the account form that what you want is steady income and safety of principle, and on the recommendation of your broker, you purchase stock which does not suit you, then the account form can be used to illustrate your investment goals. Your broker should have realized from the account form that you may have

been unsuited for that particular type of investment.
SAVINGS: A lot of aggravation and possibly money.

8. **BEWARE!** Many stockbrokers after you explain your needs may recommend what is known as a proprietary product. This could be a mutual fund, or other product, that is sold by the brokerage firm salesman, as well as managed by the brokerage firm itself. Such products enable the firm to make both a commission from selling it, and a continuing fee from managing it. As a result, the firm gives the salesman an incentive to sell these products rather than other products. The incentive may be in the form of higher payouts of commission or special gifts if they sell a certain amount. Before you buy any proprietary product, ask your salesman to show you its track record (performance record) for the past one, three, five, and ten years, if possible. You should then compare it to other investments in the same category, and this way you can judge if your salesman s recommendation is truly in your best interest.

9. Clients often ask if the sales load charged when they bought a mutual fund is tax deductible as an expense. The answer is

that it usually is not, but there is a strategy. What you can do is to buy a fund in a family of funds which allows switching from one fund to another. Switching is actually a buy and a sell. If you invest $10,000.00 in a fund with a six percent sales load, the net asset value (N.A.V.) is actually only $9,400.00. If you wait a month and then switch to the fund you actually want, you will switch at N.A.V., which, depending on the N.A.V. at that time could give you a short term loss. Because the government changes the tax laws so often, you should call your accountant to see if this is still possible; if it is, you may be able to save a lot of money.

Update 2002

The greatest tool that can help you save money today when buying or selling securities is the internet. The average investor has access to almost any information relation to stocks, bonds, or mutual funds. Since I'm an investment counselor for my clients when I want to find out about a mutual fund I start at www.morningstar.com. That website will give me enough vital information to continue my due diligence to get additional information. I also use www.google.com as my main search engine. I just type in any name of a stock, bond or fund and it gets me there.

CHAPTER 6

ARBITRATION

Many customers who have had claims against brokerage firms have won financial awards. In 1989, there were more than 2800 decisions made by arbitrators on customer complaints, and over 1500 of them received a financial award. This means that over 53% of all customer claims decided in 1989 resulted in financial awards.

In 1990, the results were even better. Over 58% of the claimants won a financial award. This does not include all the cases that are settled prior to the arbitration panel making a decision. Almost 50% of the arbitration cases are settled before a decision is made. This means 75%, or three out of four people who file for arbitration get back part or all of their money. In 1991, the NASD reported the number of arbitration cases soared to over 4000.

Here is a list of terms that you should know since they are the most common reasons for customer complaints in arbitration cases.

1. **Churning - ** This is where the stockbroker excessively buys and sells in an account specifically to generate commissions. It is illegal for the broker to generate trades, or churn, a clients account. Churning can usually be proven in two ways. The first is known as the "Looper Method" or turnover ratio. An example of this would be if your opening balance in your account is $100,000 and the purchases of securities in the account is $600,000, then the turnover ratio is 6:1. The next method is known as the " Goldberg Cost / Equity Maintenance Factor". This is simply determining the clients costs, or commission, of the trades. As an example, if you do ten round trip trades in a year and each buy and sell has a total commission of 3%, you need to make at least 30% on all the trades in your account just to cover costs.

2. **Misrepresentation** - This is when a broker **intentionally** omits important facts or misleads you on the risks of certain investments. *Example:* a government mutual fund does not mean the government guarantees payments made by the mutual fund. So, if the broker says it s government guaranteed he is misrepresenting the mutual fund.

3. **Unsuitability** - This is when your investments do not meet your investment profile. If your investment profile states that you

want safety of principle and conservative income, then you may be unsuited for high risk investments; i.e., certain types of option and speculative stocks and bonds. You may also be financially unsuitable for a specific investment.

4. **Unauthorized Trading** - This is when a broker trades (buy or sell) in an account without the customer giving the broker authority.

5. **Negligence** - This is when a broker or firm does not act in the customer s best interest. This could be done by not following a customer s order or omitting pertinent information on an investment.

If you have a complaint against your brokerage firm or stockbroker, the first step is to contact the branch manager as soon as possible. You should do this in writing. If you are not satisfied with the results, you should contact, in writing, the president of the brokerage firm. Again, if you are not satisfied, then your options are mediation, arbitration, or possibly, litigation. What a mediator tries to do is to bring both sides together to discuss the case and how it might be settled. Any decision made by the mediator is **NOT** binding on either party. It is only a suggestion.

Arbitration is a legal means of resolving disputes, it is binding on both parties. It is important to know that you do not need an attorney to go to arbitration. You should, however, consider at least consulting an attorney in order to find out what to expect in an arbitration hearing. If you decide to go for a consultation, look for an attorney who has arbitration experience and is familiar with securities law. If you feel you need an attorney, try to find one who will accept your case on a contingency fee basis, so that if you do not prevail and no award is granted to you, then you will only be responsible for the costs of the arbitration, and not your attorney s fees. If you want to know more about the costs and procedures of arbitration, contact the National Association of Securities Dealers (N.A.S.D.) at:

N.A.S.D. Financial Center
33 Whitehall Street
New York, New York 10004
Tel # 212/858-4000

This organization will have virtually all the information you will need, and will send it to you.

Update 2002

Before you go to arbitration there is an additional forum in the securities industry known as Mediation. In contrast to arbitration, mediation tries to get both sides to settle the dispute with an acceptable compromise to both parties. Mediators are neutrals. They don't makes any decisions or awards. It is also an informal process. The costs are less than an arbitration.

CHAPTER 7

PREPARING FOR AN ARBITRATION

If you have tried to work out an agreement with the brokerage firm over your losses but were unsuccessful and feel you have exhausted all alternatives, then you must prepare to file for arbitration. Begin with gathering all documents that relate to your account and your claim and put them in chronological order. Start from the beginning, which will probably be the opening account forms including the customer agreements. If you do not have these documents, write a letter to the branch manager of the local office and ask him to send it to you within 10 days. Do not just call on the phone, follow up with letters every week until you receive them. Go over each question on the account form: note what type of account you had - cash or margin; do you have more than one account at the brokerage firm; what investment objective was checked off; did you check them off or did the broker; was your background information completed; did you complete it or did the broker; is your birth date correct; is your prior investment history, income and net worth correct as of the time the account was opened; did you sign the account form after you answered all of the questions; did you complete the account form at home or in the broker s office; do you remember why you opened an account at that particular brokerage firm and why you chose that particular broker; did you give the broker discretion over your account - that is, did the broker initiate the trades in your account; and did you give him written authority to do so?

Next, put together all the monthly statements and trade confirmations in chronological order. Note any trades in question. Here is some advice - don t write anything on the original statements or confirmations as you will probably have to produce them for the respondents or brokerage firm. They may get additional information from these comments that you don t want them to have. Also these comments might affect your credibility to the arbitration panel.

Next, check the gross commissions on the confirmations, if you feel they were excessive, add them up by month and in total. You should understand that some confirmations will show no commissions. This happens when the brokerage firm acts as principal or market maker in a specific security. Ask the brokerage firm what profit they made on these trades. If they don t tell you, you will get it later when you ask the firm for the commission run of the broker. This a monthly statement showing how much commissions the broker made on each trade.

Next, put together any correspondence you had with the broker. Did he send you any information on specific products, research reports, prospectuses or recommendations on a specific security you invested in? Did you ever write letters to the broker or branch manager complaining about a specific investment? Did they respond in writing? After you have gathered all this information, write a detailed account of what happened to you. Use documents to verify your statements. Start from the beginning when you opened the account and put in as much detail as possible. One more thing, if there is an individual who can help you verify any information about the claim, make sure you put them in the statement. Example, were you with your spouse or a friend when you opened the account or when you and the broker had a discussion on the specific investment in question? Did your accountant ever speak to your broker? Did you ever speak to the branch manager? What was the conversation?

At this point, you may or may not decide to use an attorney. If you decide to use an attorney, your next question is how do you find one? Here are a few suggestions: One, referral from friends, acquaintances, accountants or other professional people. They may know an attorney who specializes in securities and arbitration law. Second, call the local bar association for a list of attorneys specializing in this type of law. Choose one or two and call them for a consultation. At this stage, it is worth paying for their time to find one you are comfortable with. Usually, they won t charge you for the initial consultation. If,after you discuss your case, the attorney does not accept you as a client, ask him why. If he feels you do not have a good case, you may reconsider the claim. If he accepts you as a client, find out how he charges for his services. If it is an hourly charge, get a rough estimate of what that could be. The charge would vary greatly, depending on if the case is settled early on before arbitration or if you have to go through the entire arbitration process. His fee may be on a contingent fee basis. This means he will receive a percentage of the financial award, if he wins an award. Most attorneys will ask for a retainer. This will usually be a few thousand dollars. Make sure you ask what expenses are and are not covered by the retainer.

If you decide not to use an attorney, your next step is to obtain and fill out the filing forms for the arbitration. You should also receive the rules or Code of Arbitration Procedure. This booklet will tell you the costs involved to file, plus other pertinent information. The first form you will fill out is the Statement of Claim - your name, the brokerage firm s name, the dollar amount in dispute and the relief requested, issues to be determined by the arbitrators - in other words, your side of the story. Be specific, put in as much detail in chronological order and copies of documents to verify your claim against the brokerage firm and the broker. Show as strong as possible why they should be responsible and not you for your losses. Also put in the total amount of damages you request, such as attorneys fees or punitive damages. Remember, you have to prove to the arbitrators that you are right and the brokerage firm was wrong. Also, don t grossly overstate your damages. You filing fees are based on damages claimed and your credibility may be affected if you overly exaggerate your damages. You will I also fill I out a cover sheet for your statement of claim that will only be used by the forum staff.

ARBITRATORS

If you have a panel of three arbitrators, one will be affiliated with the securities industry. The other two will be public arbitrators from outside the securities industry. You will be entitled to the names and employment histories of the arbitrators, plus you may request copies of all awards rendered in previous arbitrations by these arbitrators. This could show a preference or a conflict of interest of a specific arbitrator. If you object to a specific arbitrator for good cause, they will probably be replaced.
Once you file the Statement of Claim and the

brokerage firm answers the claim, you may want additional documents from the brokerage firm. Make sure your request is in writing. Request the following documents (even if you already have them):

(1) Opening account forms.

(2) Customer agreements.

(3) Option agreements.

(4) Margin agreements.

(5) Any and all documents you have ever signed. These documents usually will show suitability for and your awareness of specific investments.

(6) Monthly account statements and confirmations. These documents will show trading activity in the account. This could be important if the claim is for suitability, churning or unauthorized trading.

(7) The brokerage firm's compliance manuals and/or account executive manuals. This can be useful if the broker did not follow specific standards that are required by the brokerage firm. Also may show that the firm did not adequately supervise the account executive.

(8) Forms U-4 and U-5. The U-4 is filled out by the broker when he is hired by the firm. This form will show any disciplinary history or claims filed against the account executive. The U-5 is filled out and gives the reasons why and when the broker leaves the firm. Was it voluntary or involuntary. Also try to get the U-5 from the broker s previous firms.

(9) **Due diligence reports.** This is information the brokerage firm puts together after researching facts on a specific company or product that they recommend. These facts may prove stability,untrue statements,or misrepresentations made by the broker for you to invest in this product.

(10) **Prospectuses and sales literature.** This could show suitability for a recommended investment by the broker. Also possible omission of facts and misrepresentations.

(11) **Account executive holding page and order tickets.** Holding page shows the activity of the account by the broker. This could be used to show churning, unauthorized trading or failure to supervise. Order tickets show the exact time the order was put in to be executed. You might prove the broker called you in the afternoon, convinced and recommended that you buy a specific investment when he actually bought it for you in the morning.

(12) **Commission runs for your account.** This could show excessive commissions charged to your account.

You should also remember that the brokerage firm has the right to request documents from you to prove their case. Brokerage firms do not want to give you back money. They are going to do whatever is necessary to prove you were knowledgeable about the investment. Here is a list of typical documents requested by brokerage firms:

(I)   **Federal and other income tax returns.** This could help them in knowing your financial status.

(2)   **Loan applications.** This could show financial ability and financial history.

(3)   **Any correspondence the brokerage firm sent you.** These documents could show your awareness of certain investments and activity.

(4)   **Other brokerage firm's account applications and activities.** These will show what type of information and trading activity you are doing at another firm.

(5)   **Your resume.** This will show education, business experience, memberships to organizations or clubs. This could show the type of sophistication and knowledge on certain investments.

(6)   **Lists of subscriptions to publications, newsletters and clubs.** This could show knowledge to certain investments.

Another fact you should know is that there are public sources where you can obtain information on brokerage firm s personnel, the branch manager and the broker. The main source is the **Central Registration Depository (CRD).** You may obtain any disciplinary records, awards or settlements by brokerage firms or their brokers, plus biographical and licensing data. The telephone number is (301) 590-6500. If you care to write to them, their address is: NASD/CRD, 9513 Key West Avenue, Rockville, Maryland 20850.

After you have prepared the next step is the hearing. The chairperson will formally open the hearing and administer an oath to all parties and witnesses. You will have your opening statement. This will be what you intend to prove. This should be concise and well planned. The respondent will do the same. Then you will present your case. The opposing side has the right to object to your documents and evidence.

At that point, the arbitrators will ask why they are objecting to your evidence. After the explanation, the panel may acceptor reject the objection. If you have a witness to help your case, the respondents have a right to cross-examine them. The respondents will try to reduce the damage his testimony has brought or they may try to damage his credibility. When you finish your presentation of your allegations, documents and witnesses, the respondent will present its case. Remember, you also have the right to object to their evidence and witnesses. You also have the right to cross-examine their witnesses. When the respondent finishes its case, the panel has a right to ask additional questions of either party or witnesses. If there are no more questions or witnesses, then both parties are allowed closing arguments. Your closing argument should show what you believe your evidence and witnesses have proved and what the respondent s evidence and witnesses failed to prove against you. The arbitrators will try to render a decision for an award within thirty (30) days. You may or may not win and the arbitrators do not have to give a reason for their decision.

Update 2002

When preparing for an arbitration go to www.nasdadr.com. You will be able to get all the forms. You can also get different arbitration cases that could relate to your case to review. you can also get the brokers U4. This will give you past and present information on the broker.

CHAPTER 8

DID YOU BUY
MUTUAL FUNDS?

Between 1984 and 2000, the brokerage firm industry received enormous revenue for selling specific types of mutual funds. Billions of dollars of these funds were sold to the public.

Many of these funds have gone down in value. A lot of people got angry, and some even took the brokerage firms to arbitration to get their money back. Many people felt the volatility of the fund was either misrepresented to them or that their broker should have realized that they were unsuited for this type of investment.

The next pages show the decisions of arbitration cases when mutual funds were either a cause or part of the cause for the arbitration. These decisions are presented with a case summary, the relief requested, and the award granted. I have used initials instead of the actual names of the claimants, in order to protect their privacy. Since decisions and awards were not made public prior to May, 1989, there are only a small number of cases available where arbitrators made a financial award to customers.

Remember that as many as 50% of all cases between customers and brokerage firms are settled before the arbitrator makes a final decision. It should also be understood that just because one arbitration panel agrees with a customer in a specific action on a specific product, **THIS IS NOT A GUARANTEE OR PRECEDENT ON ANY OTHER ARBITRATION.** Arbitrators base their decision on the facts and merits of each case, not on other arbitration cases. At the end of the case I ve noted the reason why the claimant filed for arbitration and any important facts about the awards.

CHAPTER 9

ARBITRATION AWARDS - MUTUAL FUNDS

Claimant: B.W.F.

Respondent: Prudential Securities

Case Summary

This claim was filed on or about December 2000

Claimant asserted the following causes of action: breach of contract, negligence, and failure to execute, and breach of fiduciary duty.

Respondents denied the allegations made in the Statement of Claim. Respondent states that all times claimant had or should have had full knowledge of all material facts concerning the investment he made, including the nature of the investments and the associated risks. Claimant directed and authorized the execution of all transactions in his account. Respondents are not liable for losses because they were within the risks Claimant chose to assume.

Relief Requested

Claimant requested compensatory damages in the amount of $ 17,980.12 plus punitive damages, interest at the rate of 12%, attorney's fees, and forum fees.

Award

Prudential is solely liable for and shall pay the Claimant the sum of $10,077.20 as compensatory damages, plus interest at 12% per annum from December 21, 2000 totaling $1,612.32, for a total award of $11,689.52

Date and Place

April 11, 2001 Boston, Massachusetts

Note: Even though the Claimant should have known the risks and did authorize the transactions, the arbitration panel still found Prudential liable.

Number: 1012

Claimant: HD

Respondent: Prudential Securities

Case Summary

The case was filed July 31,2001
Claimant alleges unsuitable investments in aggressive stocks, all Internet and telecommunications related, misrepresentation, Violation of Florida State Statutes, breach of contract, negligence and failure to supervise.

Relief requested

Claimant requested $280.000.

Award

The respondent shall pay to the claimant the sum of $257,251.45, $256,501.45 as an award on the claim and $750.00 as a return of claimant's deposit of costs. The claimant prevailed on the claim under Florida Statute 517.301 and is therefore entitled to attorney's fee.

Date and Place

April 18,2002 Fort Lauderdale, Florida

Note: Claimant was unsuitable for internet and telecommunication investments. Also claimant received his attorney's fees back.

Number: 1103

Claimant: EJC & HBC

Respondent: Merrill Lynch

Case Summary
The case was filed February 5, 2002
Claimant alleged that the respondent purchased stock that was unsuitable for their age and investment objectives. Claimant maintains that due to respondent's action, the account suffered losses

Relief Requested

Claimant is asking for $25,000.00

Award

Respondent is liable and shall pay the Claimant $25,000.00.

Date and Place

August 12, 2002, Newport Beach, California

Note: What is important about this case is that first the claimants appeared pro se, which means they did it themselves without an attorney. Also they got back 100% of what they asked for. These investments were unsuitable for their age and investment objective

Number: 1130

Claimant: JB

Respondent: Salomon Smith Barney

Case Summary

The case was filed November 5, 2001
The claimant alleges that the registered representative made unauthorized trades in the account and that the account incurred substantial charges from the sale of mutual funds.

Relief Requested

Claimant requested $6,248.00

Award

Salomon Smith Barney shall pay JB $1,454.00 as an award on the Statement of Claim. Forum fees are assessed against the Respondent.

Date and Place

April 19, 2002 Philadelphia, PA.

Number: 103MF

Claimants: L.M. and J.M.

Respondent: E.F. Hutton & Company, Inc. and J.Sm.

AWARD

1. Respondents E.F. Hutton & Company, Inc. and J.S. are jointly and severally liable for and shall pay to the Claimants the sum of Seven Thousand, Nine Hundred, Eight-Four Dollars and Four Cents ($7,984.04) which represents commissions charged by Respondent for improperly switching Claimants' funds from the Putnam Hi Income Government Trust to the Hutton Government Securities Series, a change which did not result in significant or material benefit to Claimants.

2. Respondents E.F. Hutton & Company, Inc. and J.S. are jointly and severally liable for and shall pay to the Claimants the sum of $400.00 (Four Hundred Dollars and Zero Cents) representing payment of the filing fee previously deposited with the National Association of Securities Dealers, Inc. by Claimant.

DATE

December 8, 1988

NOTE: Stockbroker switching a client from one load fund to another load fund without reasonable benefit to the client.

Number: 104MF

Claimants: R. & D. T.

Respondents: Piper, Jaffray & Hopwood, Inc. and S.F.

SUMMARY OF ISSUES

This case was filed on September 20, 1988. Claimants Alleged misrepresentation in the purchase of shares of a mutual fund, Keystone Tax Free Fund.

Respondents denied the allegations of Claimants and alleged the following affirmative defenses: claims barred by the applicable statutes of limitation; laches; failure to state a claim upon which relief can be granted; respondents acted in good faith; damages allegedly suffered have no causal relationship with any act or omission attributable to respondents; failure to mitigate damages; claimants did not reasonable rely on any act or omission of respondents; waiver.

DAMAGES AND RELIEF REQUESTED

Claimants requested compensatory damages of $7,215.56
Respondents requested costs and disbursements.

DAMAGES AND RELIEF AWARDED

1. Respondents are jointly and severally liable for and shall pay to claimants the sum of $5,772.45 in compensatory damages.

2. The parties shall each bear their respective costs including attorneys' fees.

NOTE: Misrepresented facts about a mutual fund. What is important about this case is the broker says the client waited too long to file the claim.

Number: 105MF

Claimants: I. & M. N.

Respondents: Comm Vest Securities, Inc.

CASE SUMMARY

This claim was filed with the NASD, Inc. on May 26, 1989. The hearing was conducted in Fort Lauderdale, Florida on February 13, 1990 with a total of one (1) session.

Claimants, I. and M. N. ("N"), alleged that Respondent, CommVest Securities, Inc. ("CommVest"), recommended the purchase of Putnam High Income Government Trust as a "no risk" safe investment, to preserve principal, earn 12% interest and quarterly dividend checks; that through its broker, R. M., CommVest made misrepresentations of material facts and omitted to state material facts; and, used high pressure to sell Claimants on unsuitable investment.

Respondent denied all allegations of wrongdoing; alleged that it fully and truthfully advised the Claimants about the Putnam investment from the Putnam documents; that the investment appeared to be suitable in providing a stable income for retirees; that Putnam's own mismanagement may have caused the demise of the fund; that Claimants are not novice investors and made a voluntary and informed purchase of the fund at issue.

RELIEF REQUESTED

Claimants requested damages in the amount of $50,000.00 for the value their investment would have been worth today (principal plus interest). Respondent requested dismissal of the claim and an award in favor of CommVest.

AWARD

1. Respondent, CommVest, is hereby liable and shall pay to Claimants the amount of Eleven Thousand and 00/100 ($11,000.00) Dollars inclusive of interest.

DATE

February 13, 1990

NOTE: Misrepresented and omitted facts about government fund. What is important about case is that the brokerage firm tries to put the blame on the fund's management itself. Also brokerage firm says client was knowledgeable investor and should have known the risks.

Number: 106MF

Claimant: R. K.

Respondent: Dreyfus Service Corporation

1. Within thirty (30) days from the date of transmittal of this Award to the Parties, DREYFUS SERVICE CORPORATION hereinafter referred to as RESPONDENT, shall pay to R. K., hereinafter referred to as CLAIMANT, the sum of SIXTEEN THOUSAND EIGHT HUNDRED TWENTY SIX DOLLARS AND EIGHTY CENTS ($16,826.80), plus interest thereon at the rate of 9% per annum from the date of June 25, 1987 to the date of payment.

2. Within thirty (30) days from the date of transmittal of this Award to the Parties, RESPONDENT shall also pay to CLAIMANT the sum of FIFTY THOUSAND DOLLARS ($50,000.00), representing punitive damages.

3. With respect to all other claims of CLAIMANT against RESPONDENT, same are denied in their entirety.

4. The compensation of the Arbitrator totalling ONE THOUSAND FIVE HUNDRED DOLLARS ($1,500.00), shall be borne equally by the Parties.

DATE AND PLACE

June 25, 1987 in New York

NOTE: What is important about this award is that arbitrators agreed to punitive damages.

71

Number: 107MF

Claimants: G. & M. H.

Respondent: Shearson Lehman Hutton, Inc.

CASE SUMMARY

Date filed: 8/1/89

First scheduled: 12/21/89

Customer v. member firm: misrepresentation in failing to advise that proprietary fund shares were not transferable, $25,348.88 redemption fee.

RELIEF REQUESTED

Claim: $63,635.47; Punitive: $15,000.00; Atty fees: $5,000.00; Deposit: $400.00

AWARD

The Respondent Shearson Lehman Hutton, Inc. shall pay to Claimant G. & M. J. H. Foundation the total sum of $69,035.47 which represents $63,635.47 an award on the claim, $5,000.00 as attorney fees and $400.00 as Claimants' refund of the deposit of costs. Also, the additional costs in the $400.00 is assessed against the Respondent Shearson Lehman Hutton, Inc.

DATE AND PLACE

December 21, 1989 in Houston, Texas

NOTE: Case shows proprietary fund (fund which is sold and managed by the firm) could not be transferred.

Number: 108MF

Claimants: W. & D. J.

Respondents: McLaughlin, Piven, Vogel, Inc.

CASE SUMMARY

Date filed: 7/21/89

First scheduled: 12/13/89

Decided: 12/13/89.

Customer alleges that they were misinformed regarding the volatility of the Franklin Fund

RELIEF REQUESTED

$1,300.00

AWARD

$1,000.00

The Claimant is to receive from Respondent $1,025.00. $1,000.00 representing the award, and $25.00 representing the costs assessed. Costs are assessed against the Respondent.

DATE AND PLACE

December 13, 1989 in New York City, NY

NOTE: Broker misinformed them of the volatility. Also it was worth going to arbitration for as little as $1300.00.

Number: 109MF

Claimant: D. E.

Respondent: Shearson Lehman Hutton, Inc. and D. B.

CASE SUMMARY

Customer vs. member firm and registered representative. Claimant alleges she is ill and invested $125,000.00 in Hutton Investment Securities to meet her stated investment objectives of preservation of principal and a 12% return. Claimant further alleges that her broker highly recommended that she transfer her funds to the Colonial Tax Exempt High Yield Fund which resulted in a penalty.

AWARD REQUESTED

$10,624.00

AWARD

$9,502.92

The Respondents, Shearson Lehman Hutton, Inc, and D. B., are hereby jointly and severally liable to pay to the Claimant the sum of $9,902.92, representing an award on the claim in the amount of $9,502.92, and a return of Claimant's deposit of costs of $400.00.

The claim was originally scheduled for a hearing. However, due to Claimant's illness the parties agreed to submit the matter for a determination based on the pleadings.

DATE AND PLACE

December 8, 1989 in New York City, NY

NOTE: Switching from one load fund to another load fund without reasonable benefit to client.

Number: 110MF

Claimants: A. & J. F.

Respondent: Shearson Lehman Hutton, Inc.

CASE SUMMARY

Date filed: 4/13/89

First scheduled: 7/25/89

Decided: 11/13/89

Customer v. Member Firm - alleges misrepresentation and unsuitability regarding investment in Government Fund.

RELIEF REQUESTED

$10,000.00

AWARD

$2,131.80

Respondent shall pay to claimant the total sum of $2,331.80 which represents an award on the claim in the amount of $2,131.80 and a reimbursement of $200.00 representing claimant's deposit.

DATE AND PLACE

November 13, 1989 in New York city, NY

NOTE: Misrepresented facts about government fund.

Number: 111MF

Claimant: W. R. and B. R.

Respondents: Merrill Lynch, Pierce, Fenner & Smith, Inc. and R. B.

CASE SUMMARY

This claim was filed with the NASD, Inc. on June 16, 1988. The hearing was conducted in Tampa, Florida on August 15, 1989 and September 19, 1989 with a total   of six (6) sessions.

Claimants W. R. and B. R. ("the R's) alleged that Respondents Merrill Lynch, Pierce, Fenner & Smith, Inc. ("Merrill") and R. B. ("B"): failed to follow the trading instructions of the Claimants; executed unauthorized trades in Claimants' account and engaged in a fraudulent course of conduct to conceal Respondents' failure to follow trading instructions and the unauthorized trades. Respondents denied liability and alleged that: the losses suffered were beyond Respondents' control; Claimants either authorized or ratified all trades; Claimants have waived or are estopped from claiming unauthorized trades and Claimants actual losses were less than those asked for in the Statement of Claim.

RELIEF REQUESTED

Claimants requested damages in the amount of $167,943.31 plus interest, punitive damages, attorney's fees and other costs. Respondents requested dismissal of the claim and other costs.

77

AWARD

1. Respondent Merrill is hereby liable and shall pay to Claimants the following amounts:

a. For Respondent Merrill's failure to sell Claimants' ML Eurofund mutual fund on October 16, 1987, the sum of Forty Seven Thousand Seventy and 31/100 ($47,070.31) Dollars plus interest at the legal rate of 12% per annum from October 16, 1987 to the date of payment of this Award.

b. For Respondent Merrill's failure to sell Claimants' ML Natural Resources Trust mutual fund on October 9, 1987, the sum of Nine Thousand Two Hundred Seventy-Five and 42/100 ($9,275.42) Dollars plus interest at the legal rate of 12% per annum from October 9, 1987 to the date of payment of this Award.

2. Respondent Merrill is hereby liable and shall, to the extent it has not already done so, credit Claimants' account: Four Thousand Five Hundred Fifty and 40/100 ($4,550.40) Dollars for the Capital Fund mutual fund; Four Thousand Two Hundred Eighty-Six and 59/100 ($4,286.59) Dollars for the International Holdings mutual fund; and Four Thousand Six Hundred Twelve and 50/100 ($4,612.50) Dollars for the Basic Value mutual fund.

DATE

February 16, 1990

NOTE: Broker failed to follow client's instruction and did unauthorized trade in accounts.

78

Number: 112MF

Claimant: H. F.

Respondents: Easter Kramer Group Securities, Inc. and C. H.

CASE SUMMARY

This claim was filed with the NASD, Inc. on September 26, 1988. The hearing was conducted in Fort Lauderdale, Florida on October 17, 1989 with a total of two (2) sessions.

The Claimant, H. F. ("F") alleged that Respondent, Easter Kramer Group Securities, Inc. ("Easter Kramer") and C. H. were liable for damages sustained by: Respondents' failure to inform Claimant of a price break and letter of intent which he was entitled to: failure to provide Claimant with a switch letter that would have advised him that he would have to pay a further commission when he switched the funds and failure to inform Claimant of the disadvantages of buying different families of funds. Also, claimant alleged: that the second switch was into an unsuitable fund and that Respondents were liable for fraud and negligence. Respondents asserted the affirmative defenses of: good faith; waiver; estoppel; laches and lack of proximate cause. Additionally, Respondents alleged that: Claimant had failed to set forth allegations to support an award of punitive damages; H acted in compliance with all applicable rules and regulations; Respondents were not negligent or reckless and Claimant never informed Respondents that he would be investing over $100,000.00 which would have entitled him to the price break.

79

AWARD

D. E., representative of Easter Kramer, told staff attorney, A. F. on October 16, 1989 via telephone, that he did not plan on attending the hearing and that, therefore, Easter Kramer would not have a representative there.

1. Respondents are hereby liable, jointly and severally, and shall pay to Claimant the amount of One Thousand Three Hundred Five and 76/100 ($1,305.76) Dollars inclusive of interest at the legal rate of 12% per annum.

DATE

October 17, 1989

NOTE: Breakpoints. It is also important when switching from one fund to another. Client must be told of the cost. This is done by a switch letter.

Number: 113MF

Claimant: R. S.

Respondent: Hyder & Co., Inc. and John Nuveen & Co.

CASE SUMMARY

Claimant R. S. alleged that Respondents Hyder & Co., Inc. and John Nuveen & Co. failed to execute a sales transaction at the quoted price. Respondent John Nuveen & Co., Inc. maintains that Claimant received the appropriate redemption price for the securities sold and denies having provided Claimant with the higher quotations alleged by Claimant. Respondent Hyder & Co., Inc. maintains that Respondent Nuveen & Co., Inc. confirmed the sale of the subject securities at a higher price than that which was subsequently received by Claimant. Respondent Hyder & Co., Inc. further maintains that it cannot be held liable for the false quotation by Respondent Nuveen & Co., Inc. and its failure to rectify the trade.

RELIEF REQUESTED

Claimant R. S. requested damages of Four Thousand Eight Hundred Thirty Five Dollars and No Cents ($4,835.00) plus interest. Respondents requested dismissal of claim and costs.

AWARD

That Respondent John Nuveen & Co., Inc. is separately liable and shall pay to the

Claimant the sum of Four Thousand Eight Hundred Fifteen Dollars and No Cents ($4,815.00), and;

That the claim against Hyder & Co., Inc. is hereby dismissed in all respects.

DATE

March 15, 1990

NOTE: Client was given a wrong quote on the price he would receive when he sold his bonds.

Number: 114MF

Claimant: C. B. a.k.a. S. K.

Respondents: Oppenheimer & Co., Inc., Bear Stearns & Co., Inc. and S. G.

SUMMARY OF ISSUES

Claimant alleged that Respondents breached their fiduciary duty to her, failed to supervise account executive G, and defrauded her by placing 75% of her irreplaceable assets in unsuitable managed commodities funds, by placing her remaining funds in a stock account and trading excessively in unsuitable options and misrepresenting to Claimant the high risk of loss involved with trading options. Claimant further alleged Respondent G. misrepresented the suitability and risk potential of certain limited partnership investments which he recommended and which were not Oppenheimer products.

Respondents denied Claimant's allegations and asserted that Claimant was a sophisticated investor with previous securities investment experience who wanted to trade aggressively in spectulative investments. Respondents also maintained that claimant dissuade with Respondent G. the investment strategy prior to trading, that claimant signed numerous risk disclosure statements and other documents affirming her acceptance of risk.

DAMAGES AND RELIEF REQUESTED

83

Claimant requested damages, amended at hearing, of $167,000.00 plus interest at 10% against Respondents Oppenheimer & Co., Inc. and S. G. Claimant requested damages of $26,000.00 plus interest against Respondent G. only. Claimant also requested punitive damages in the amount of $2,000,000.00 and an award of costs of arbitration.

AWARD

Respondents Oppenheimer and G. are jointly and severally liable for and shall pay to Claimant the sum of One Hundred Thousand Dollars and Zero Cents ($100,000.00) only.

2. Respondent G. is individually liable for and shall pay to Claimant the sum of Twenty-Six Thousand Dollars and Zero Cents ($26,000.00) only.

3. The claim for punitive damages is dismissed.

4. The parties shall each bear their respective costs including attorneys' fees.

5. In accordance with Section 43 of the NASD Code of Arbitration Procedure, the NASD shall retain the $1,000.00 filing fee previously deposited by the Claimant. Respondents Oppenheimer and G. are jointly and severally assessed $4,000.00 in forum fees, as follows:

  a. $3,000.00 payable to the National Association of Securities Dealers, Inc.;

  b. $1,000.00 payable to the Claimant as reimbursement for the previously deposited filing fee.

OTHER ISSUES

The claim against Bear Stearns & Co., Inc. was settled prior to the hearing. Bear Stearns & Co., Inc. was then dismissed as a Respondent in this matter.

DATE AND PLACE

July 20, 1990 In Los Angeles, California

NOTE: Suitability. Broker was individually liable.

Number: 115MF

Claimants: W. & F. S.

Respondents: Merrill Lynch, Pierce, Fenner & Smith, Inc. and P.S.

CASE SUMMARY

Claimants W. and F. S., alleged that Respondents took their order to sell a mutual fund approximately 20 to 25 minutes before the market closed on October 16, 1987, and did not advise Claimants that there might be a problem in effecting the transaction that day. In fact, that did not effect the transaction that day, but did so the next day, so that the Claimants experienced a decrease in the amount of proceeds from the sale in the amount of $3,186.83.

Respondents maintained that while they did take the order, the Claimants were advised that it might be difficult to effect the transaction that day, and it would be effected the next day if the difficulty arose.

RELIEF REQUESTED

Claimants requested the sum of $3,186.83 being the difference between the closing price on the mutual funds sold on October 16, 1987 and October 19, 1987.

AWARD

Respondents are liable to the Claimants and shall pay to the Claimants the sum of Three Thousand One Hundred Eighty Six and Eighty Three Cents ($3,186.83); no interest is awarded on this amount.

DATE AND PLACE

February 28, 1990 in Louisville, Kentucky

NOTE: Depending on the family of funds, switching may be required 1-2 hours prior to end of trading day.

Number: 116MF

Claimant: A & R K

Respondents: Shearson Lehman Brothers, Inc. and E. F.

CASE SUMMARY

In a claim filed with the National Association of Securities Dealers, Inc. on June 6, 1988, Claimant A & R K Realty alleged the Respondents misrepresented the yield the Claimant would receive on its investment in the Shearson Lehman Brothers, Inc. Special Tax Exempt Income Portfolio and told the Claimant the investment would provide complete portfolio liquidity and misrepresented to the Claimant that the investment did not contain any fees for redemption upon liquidation of the fund. Respondents Shearson Lehman Brothers, Inc. and E. F. maintained they never "guaranteed" a fixed yield to the Claimant and the Claimant as an experienced and ultra sophisticated investor knew no guarantee existed and further maintained Respondents never represented to the Claimant that there were no redemption fees upon liquidation. Respondents Shearson Lehman Brothers, Inc. and E. F. further maintained any losses incurred were the result of Claimant's own deliberate and informed investment decisions.

RELIEF REQUESTED

Claimant requested damages of $37,000.00. Respondents requested dismissal of claim plus costs.

AWARD

The Respondent Shearson Lehman Bothers, Inc. be and hereby is liable and shall pay to the claimant A & R K the sum of Twenty Four Thousand Dollars and No Cents

($24,000.00), inclusive of interest.

DATE AND PLACE

March 14, 1990 in New York City, New York

NOTE: Misrepresentation. Also Shearson says claimant was "experienced and ultra sophisticated investor.

Number: 117MF

Claimants: C. & T. M.

Respondents: Thomson McKinnon Securities, Inc. and G. W.

CASE SUMMARY

Claimants C. & T. M. (Hereinafter "Claimants") alleged that Respondents Thomson McKinnon Securities, Inc. (hereinafter "TMS") and G. W. (hereinafter "W") placed Claimants in an unsuitable investment. Claimants alleged that they invested in National Municipal Trust Insured Series 16 and that Respondents failed to deliver a prospectus for that Trust in a timely fashion. Claimants further alleged that W made misrepresentations concerning the Claimants' investment and in the commissions that the Respondents would receive for the investment.

Respondents maintained that the investment was fully and accurately discussed with the Claimants and that W provided the claimants and their accountant with prospectus soon after the purchase. Respondents maintained that the investment was suitable for the Claimants and categorically deny all allegations in claimants' claim.

RELIEF REQUESTED

Claimants requested damages in the amount of $272,260.00 and their attorney fees in connection with their arbitration. Thomson McKinnon Securities, Inc. and G. W. requested that the arbitrators dismiss the Claimants' claim in its entirety and assesses the cost of the proceeding against the Claimants.

89

AWARD

The Claimants C. & T. M. shall recover $39,835.00 from Thomson McKinnon Securities, Inc., and $19,917.00 from G. W.; payable $39,835.00 to C. M. and $19,917.00 to T. M.

2. The parties shall each bear their respective costs including attorney fees.

DATE AND PLACE

February 28, 1990 in Louisville, Kentucky

NOTE: Misrepresented investment and concessions.   Did not receive prospectus in a timely fashion.

Number: 121MF

Claimant: B. H.

Respondents: Shearson Lehman Hutton, Inc. and C. K.

SUMMARY OF ISSUES

Claimant filed this claim with the NASD on November 7, 1988 and alleged that the recommended investments including two limited partnerships, a real estate syndication, high yielding utility stocks, mutual funds and investment trust, were unsuitable to her investment objectives. Claimant further alleged that Respondents misrepresented the risks and terms of the investments recommended.

Respondents denied the allegations and maintained that the recommended investments were suitable to Claimant's objective of income-producing investments. Respondents further maintained that each recommended investment was fully explained and discussed with Claimant and that claimant authorized each purchase.

RELIEF REQUESTED

Claimant requested damages in the amount of $15,658.48 for losses incurred on stock investments, $15,803.00 for losses incurred on mutual fund investments and $30,000.00 as the amount invested in the two limited partnerships. Claimant further requested $20,000.00 for emotional and physical distress, punitive damages of $75,000.00 and reasonable attorneys' fees and costs.

Respondents requested dismissal of the claim.

AWARD

1. Respondents are hereby jointly and severally liable for and shall pay to claimant the sum of Twelve Thousand, Four Hundred Seventy-Five Dollars and Zero Cents ($12,475.00) based upon the finding that the limited partnership and high yielding utility stocks were not suitable, calculated as follows:

>   a. The sum of $4,733.00 representing the loss on the utility stocks; and
>   b. The sum of $7,742.00 representing the loss of income during the period of time Claimant held the limited partnership interests.

2. Respondent Shearson Lehman Hutton, Inc. shall pay to Claimant the sum of Thirty Thousand Dollars and Zero Cents ($30,000.00) which was the purchase price of the Conam and the Insured Limited Partnership interests and Claimant is directed to assign and transfer to Respondent her interest in these investments.
3. The claims for punitive damages and damages for emotional and physical distress are denied.
4. The parties shall each bear their respective costs including attorneys' fees.

DATE AND PLACE

October 19, 1989 in Los Angeles, California

NOTE: Misrepresented risks and terms of investment. Also Shearson cancelled the purchase of the limited partnership and returned full purchase price.

Number: 122MF

Claimant: D. & L. S.

Respondents: Prudential-Bache Securities, Inc. and J. K.

CASE SUMMARY

Date filed: 12/31/88

First scheduled: 9/19/90

Decided: 1/12/90

Claimants allege they retained Respondent broker to rollover a retirement fund containing 1951 shares of Tucson Electric Power Stock. Claimants further allege Respondent did successfully rollover two funds (Washington Mutual and American Capital) but failed to rollover a third fund, Massachusetts Financial.

RELIEF REQUESTED

$29,000.00

AWARD

$24,800.00

The Respondent, Prudential-Bache Securities, Inc. shall pay to the Claimants the sum of $24,800.00, representing an award on the claim inclusive of attorney's fees and interest; the costs, $800.00, be and hereby are assessed against the Respondent, Prudential-Bache Securities, Inc.

DATE AND PLACE

January 12, 1990 in Phoenix, Arizona

NOTE: Failure of broker to follow instructions.

Number: 124MF

Claimant: P. K.

Respondent: S. B.

CASE SUMMARY

Date filed: 5/31/89

First scheduled: 1/23/90

Decided: 1/23/90

Customer v. Registered Representative for alleged negligence in placing Claimant's funds in a taxable fund when a tax-free fund was requested by Claimant. Claimant also alleges that funds to be placed in Keogh account were placed in her IRA account in error.

RELIEF REQUESTED	AWARD
$8,489.47	$6,750.00

The Respondent shall pay to the Claimant the sum of $6,950.00 which represents $6,750.00 as an award on the Claimant and $200.00 as a return of Claimant's deposit of costs; furthermore, the costs of this proceeding, $400.00 are assessed against the Respondent.

REMARKS

Small claim. Claimant has requested a hearing in this matter to be conducted in Washington, D. C.

DATE AND PLACE

January 23, 1990 in Washington, D. C.

NOTE: Negligence to follow instructions.

Number: 125MF

Claimants: S. & L. P.

Respondents: Prudential-Bache Securities, Inc., Pruco Securities Corp., T. N., D. R., L. G., Prudential Insurance Company of America

CASE SUMMARY

Claimants alleged that Respondents misrepresented investments when advising Claimants to move monies from their IRA accounts at another institution to accounts governed by the Respondents. Claimants further alleged that Respondents placed them in unsuitable funds and failed to disclose the facts of and misrepresented insurance policies that were sold to them where the principles were at risk. Respondents Pruco Securities Corp., T. N., L. G. and D. R. maintained that prospectuses were provided to the Claimants and that no guarantees were ever made to the Claimants who signed applications verifying that the contract met their financial needs and objectives. Respondent Prudential-Bache Securities maintained that they were not a proper party to the proceeding. Respondent Prudential Insurance Company of America requested that they be dismissed as a party and asserted that they were not a proper respondent to the complaint.

AWARD

1. The Motion to Dismiss of Prudential Insurance Company to dismiss the firm as party is denied.

2. As decided by this panel at the hearing on November 14, 1989, the Motion to Dismiss of Prudential-Bache Securities, Inc. to dismiss Prudential-Bache Securities, Inc. as a party to this proceeding is granted.

3. Pruco Securities Corp., Prudential Insurance Company of American and D. R. shall be jointly and severally liable and shall pay to the Claimants the sum of Eleven Thousand Six Hundred Eighty Dollars and Seventy-Five Cents ($11,680.75) inclusive of interest.

4. The claims of the Claimants against T. N. and L. G. are hereby dismissed.

DATE AND PLACE

November 14, 1989 in Buffalo, New York

NOTE: Misrepresented investments, suitability.

Number: 126MF

Claimant: T. S.

Respondents: Merrill Lynch, Pierce, Fenner & Smith, Inc., and M. L.

CASE SUMMARY

Claimant T. S. alleged that he wanted to open an IRA account with the Respondent Merrill Lynch, Pierce, Fenner & Smith, Inc., namely the Merrill Lynch Federal Securities Trust Fund. Claimant alleged that Respondent M. L. guaranteed that no commissions would be charged on the purchase of this Fund. Claimant further alleged that Respondent L. never purchased this Fund for his account, but instead purchased the Merrill Lynch Retirement Income Fund. Claimant alleged he then informed Respondent L. to close the Fund and return his monies, for which the Claimant was charged a commission. Claimant also alleged that he purchased shares in the Merrill Lynch Hubbard Income Realty Partnership VI, and was assured by Respondent L. of the investment's complete liquidity. Claimant alleged he ordered the sale of this investment, and that the Respondents to date have not done so.

Respondents Merrill Lynch and M. L. denied any and all allegations of wrongdoing or liability in the Claimant's claim for damages. Respondents maintained the Claimant was fully informed that a commission would be charged on the purchase of the Federal Securities Trust Fund, and that Respondent L. purchased the Retirement Income Fund for Claimant instead because he knew of claimant's desire to avoid commissions. Moreover, Respondents contended the Claimant received a prospectus on the Merrill Lynch Hubbard Income Realty Partnership VI, and was fully apprised of the risks involved with this investment. Respondents further contended that they acted properly and that the Claimant authorized all trades.

97

RELIEF REQUESTED

Claimant T. S. requested that his Merrill Lynch Hubbard Income Realty Partnership VI fund be closed and his $2,000.00 investment returned to him, plus $454.97 in damages. Respondents Merrill Lynch, Pierce, Fenner & Smith, Inc. and M. L. requested dismissal of the claim in its entirety, plus costs.

AWARD

1. Because this panel is convinced by the testimony of Mr. S. and Mr. L. that Mr. S. never understood the particulars of the investments which Mr. L. proposed to sell him, the panel finds that:

    a. Claimant T. S. is entitled to the rescission of his Two Thousand Dollars and No Cents ($2,000.00) investment in the Merrill Lynch Hubbard Income Realty Partnership VI, and Respondent Merrill Lynch, Pierce, Fenner & Smith, Inc. be and hereby is ordered and directed to take whatever steps are necessary to extract Mr. S. from this partnership, and to pay to him forthwith the sum of Two Thousand Dollars and No Cents ($2,000.00), without interest.

    b. Respondent Merrill Lynch, Pierce, Fenner & Smith, Inc. be and hereby is liable and shall pay to the Claimant Three Hundred and Eighty-Three Dollars and Eighty Two Cents ($383.82).

2. All claims against Respondent M. L. be and hereby are dismissed in their entirety.

3. The parties each shall bear their respective costs including attorney's fees.

DATE AND PLACE

December 14, 1989 in New York City, New York

NOTE: Misrepresented fees and negligence about other facts. Arbitrators convinced claimant never understood investment.

98

Number: 127MF

Claimant: N. N. P. T.

Respondent: Gilbraltar Securities Company

CASE SUMMARY

Claimant N. N. P. T. alleged that on October 1, 1987 it instructed Respondent Gilbraltar Securities Company to liquidate its investment in the Putnam Option Income Trust II Fund. Claimant alleged that Respondent negligently failed to liquidate this Fund in a timely manner, and due to this negligence the Fund was not liquidated until October 20, 1987.

Respondent Gilbraltar Securities Company contended that liquidation of this Fund required a signed and guaranteed liquidation letter from the Claimant, and, if the account was a corporate account as in this case, a Certificate of Incumbency or valid corporate resolution. Respondent contended that any delay in the liquidation of this account was directly attributable to Putnam Investors Company's delay in providing the Respondent with the appropriate forms needed to liquidate this account. Moreover, Respondent maintained that they acted properly and in a timely manner.

AWARD

1. Respondent Gilbraltar Securities Company be and hereby is liable and shall pay to the Claimant N. N. P. T. the sum of Two Thousand Dollars and No Cents ($2,000.00), inclusive of interest.

2. The parties shall each bear their respective costs including attorney's fees.

DATE AND PLACE

December 27, 1989 in New York City, New York

NOTE: Failed to liquidate fund in a timely manner

Number: 128MF

Claimant: A. V. & D. V.

Respondent: Gruntal & Company, Inc.

CASE SUMMARY

Claimants A. & D. V. alleged that they opened an Individual Retirement Account with Respondent Gruntal & Co., Inc. through one of their account executives. Claimants alleged that they were initially put into a low risk and completely liquid fund, Alliance Capital Reserve Money Market Fund. Claimants further alleged that they were subsequently taken out of this investment and placed into Southmark CRCA Fund VI on the recommendation of the Respondent. Claimants alleged that this was a highly risky investment with virtually no liquidity, and it was thus an unsuitable investment for them. Moreover, Claimants maintained that they were never informed of the risks inherent with this investment.

Respondent denied all of the Claimants' allegations. Respondent maintained that the Claimants were informed that the investment was a limited partnership and of the risks involved. Respondent also maintained that the investment was not "inherently risky", and was a suitable investment for the Claimants.

RELIEF REQUESTED

Claimants A. & D. V. requested actual damages of $4,270.00, plus costs. Respondent Gruntal & Co., Inc. requested that the claim be dismissed in it entirety, plus costs.

AWARD

1. Respondent Gruntal & Co., Inc. be and hereby is liable and shall pay to the Claimants A. & D. V., collectively, the sum of Four Thousand Dollars and No Cents ($4,000.00), inclusive of interest.

2. Claimants A. & D. V. shall remit to Respondent Gruntal & Co., Inc. the four (4) units of Southmark CRCA Fund VI purchased for their accounts in April, 1987.

3. The parties shall each bear their respective costs including attorney's fees.

DATE AND PLACE

November 28, 1989 in New York City, New York

NOTE: Misrepresented facts and risks.

Number: 129MF

Claimants: B., R., & D. C.

Respondent: Merrill Lynch, Pierce, & Smith

Cross-Respondent: A. K.

CASE SUMMARY

This case was filed on July 11, 1988. This proceeding arises from various purchases of Putnam High Income Government Trust, some of which were on margin, in three accounts maintained by the claimants with Merrill Lynch, the Respondent. Claimants contended that Merrill Lynch's registered representative, Mr. K., failed adequately to explain the nature and risks of the investment; made purchases on margin without authorization and placed the claimants' funds in an investment which was inconsistent with the investment objective they expressed. Respondent Merrill Lynch denied Claimants' allegations and asserted that if it had any liability to the Claimants, said liability was due to the fault of Mr. K. Mr. K. denied all allegations of wrongdoing, and asserted that the transactions at issue were the results of acts by the Claimants and of another Merrill Lynch employee.

Before the hearing took place, Mr. K. moved for leave to amend his statement of answer and to assert claim against the Claimants and the Merrill Lynch employee. The arbitrators granted the motion to amend the statement of answer, and denied the motion to add claims against other parties.

103

RELIEF REQUESTED

Claimants alleged losses of $26,231.00 plus interest and $1,500.00 in legal fees. Merrill Lynch, Pierce, Fenner & Smith asserted that claimants are entitled to recover nothing, and that in the event Claimants establish they are entitled to any recovery, that A. K. should be liable for any and all such sums. Merrill Lynch also sought costs and attorneys fees from the Claimants, or, in the alternative, from Mr. K. Cross-Respondent K. requested that Merrill Lynch recover nothing on it's cross-claim, that Respondent be held liable to Mr. K. for the costs and attorneys fees of K. in this matter, and for such other and further relief as shall be deemed appropriate.

AWARD

1. Respondent Merrill Lynch, Pierce, Fenner & Smith is liable for and shall pay to Claimants the sum of Ten Thousand Seventeen Dollars and Ninety Eight Cents ($10,017.98).

2. Cross-Respondent A. K. is liable for and shall pay to Respondent Merrill Lynch, Pierce, Fenner, & Smith the sum of Ten Thousand Seventeen Dollars and Ninety Eight Cents ($10,017.98).

3. The parties shall each bear their respective costs including attorneys' fees.

DATE AND PLACE

September 6, 15 & 18, and October 6, 1989

NOTE: Misrepresented facts and unsuitable for investment objectives. Also broker did unauthorized trade.

104

Number: 130MF

Claimant: J. M.

Respondent: Prudential Bache Securities, Inc., R. G. and R. B.

CASE SUMMARY

J. M. ("Claimant") alleges that Prudential-Bache Securities, Inc. ("Respondent Bache"), R. G. ("Respondent G"), and J. R. B. ("Respondent B") (collectively referred as "Respondents") gave him "poor advice to invest in risky investments." Further, Claimant alleges that he suffered losses as a result of Respondent G's inaction on the day of the stock market "crash" in October 1987. Specifically, on October 19, 1987, Claimant allegedly requested Respondent G. to liquidate three different mutual funds and deposit the proceeds into money market accounts.

Respondents generally deny the allegations contained in the statement of claim. Specifically, the Respondents state affirmatively that Claimant ratified the transactions in his account since he received all confirmations and monthly statements from the inception of the account. Further, Claimant accepted and understood the risks involved in the recommendations given by G. Respondents allege that there are no implied or express guarantees of any kind with regards to an account executive's recommendations or advice. Respondents affirmatively state that there was no negligence or impropriety of any kind regarding the transfer of Claimant's mutual funds shares to a money market account.

105

RELIEF REQUESTED

Claimant requests damages of the amount of $13,964.00. Respondents request that the claim be dismissed in its entirety and that reasonable costs be assessed against Claimant.

AWARD

1. Respondents Prudential-Bache Securities, Inc., R. G. and J. R. B. shall pay jointly and severally to Claimant J. M. damages in the amount of Three Thousand Dollars and no/100 Cents ($3,000.00);

2. The claim for interest is denied;

3. Respondent Prudential-Bache Securities, Inc. shall pay to Claimant J. M. the sum of Four Hundred Dollars and no/100 Cents ($400.00), representing the filing fee in this matter.

DATE

January 3, 1990

Number: 131MF

Claimant: J. M. T. H.

Respondent: Dean Witter Reynolds, Inc. & C. T.

CASE SUMMARY

Customer v. Member Firm and Registered Representative - misrepresentation, unsuitable investment in bond fund, excess commission, loss of income on invested proceeds.

RELIEF AWARD

Respondents jointly and severally shall pay to the claimant the total sum of $5,500 plus interest from the date of the award at the rate of 9%. Costs are assessed against the respondents jointly and severally in the sum of $3,750.00.

DATE AND PLACE

March 8, 1990 in New York City, New York

NOTE: Misrepresentation, Suitability

Number: 132MF

Claimant: J. M.

Respondents: Shearson Lehman Hutton and M. A.

CASE SUMMARY

Date filed: 11/9/88

First scheduled: 3/15/89

Decided: 2/14/90

Customer v. Member Firm and Registered Rep alleging respondents' negligence or carelessness in failing to follow Mr. M's instructions to promptly transfer his holdings in Washington Mutual Investors Fund holdings to Cash Management Trust of America.

RELIEF REQUESTED

$62,776.00 plus interest, costs and expenses.

AWARD

Award is made in favor of Claimant J. M. and against Respondents Shearson Lehman Hutton, Inc. and M. A., jointly and severally, in the amount of $65,792.33 compensatory damages, $13,816.38 interest and $3,000.00 forum fee costs.

DATE AND PLACE

Sept. 28, 1989; Oct. 24, 1989; Nov. 17, 1989 (3 double sessions) in Rochester, NY

NOTE: Failure of broker to follow specific instructions of client.

Number: 133MF

Claimant: G. A. et. al.

Respondent: Merrill Lynch and P. L.

CASE SUMMARY

Date filed: 9/29/88

FIRST scheduled: 11/14/89

Decided: 2/13/90

Claimants' assert Respondents failed to adequately advise Claimants that the exchange of one bond fund for another would result in realized capital tax losses.

AWARD

Award: $4,500.00

Punitive: None

Atty fees: None

Costs: $750.00

Claimant shall receive $4,500.00 from Merrill Lynch. Each party shall be responsible for their own Attorney's fees and costs.

DATE AND PLACE

February 13, 1990 in Miami, Florida

NOTE: Failure to advise client switching within a family of funds is actually a buy and sell, which could realize a capital tax gain or loss.

Number: 134MF

Claimant: R. M.

Respondent: Merrill Lynch, Pierce, Fenner & Smith, Inc.

CASE SUMMARY

Claimant filed the claim on November 30, 1988. In the claim, Claimant alleged that Respondent mishandled his Basic Keogh Account by liquidating 10,904 shares of Dreyfus Fund, Inc. rather than merely transferring his shares from the "custodian" Bank of New York to the Syracuse branch office of Merrill Lynch. Respondent admitted to making the error and indicated that the error was rectified in a repurchase of the liquidated shares. The Claimant was therefore restored to his original position.

RELIEF REQUESTED

Claimant requested damages of $35,002.00, plus interest from October 5, 1987, commission earned and attorneys' fees. Respondent requested a dismissal of the claim and maintains that if the Claimant is entitled to an Award, he is entitled to no more than $6,760.48.

AWARD

A. Respondent shall be liable for and shall pay to the Claimant the sum of Thirty Five Thousand Two Dollars and No Cents ($35,002.00), without interest.

B. The parties shall each bear their respective costs, including attorneys' fees.

DATE

December 5, 1989

110

NOTE: Failure to follow specific instructions.

Number: 135MF

Claimant: K. R.

Respondent: A.G. Edwards & Sons, Inc. and E. M.

CASE SUMMARY

K. B. ("Claimant") alleged as follows:

1. E. M. ("M"), a registered representative of A. G. Edwards & Sons, Inc., (E. M. and A. G. Edwards are collectively referred to herein as "Respondents") acted as the Claimant's representative during the time period of June 16, 1982 through September 17, 1985 and engaged in the following acts or omissions:

    a. Churned the Claimant's account;

    b. Purchased unsuitable securities for the Claimant;

    c. Placed the Claimant on margin without her authorization; such margin account was unsuitable for Claimant, M. did not explain to the Claimant the risk of trading on margin; and a margin account was established for the purpose of generating more commissions;

    d. Switched the Claimant's mutual funds for other mutual funds and stock for the purpose of generating commissions;

    e. Made trades in the Claimant's account without the Claimant's authorization;

    f. Wrongfully guaranteed the price of Phibro-Salomon stock.

2. A. G. Edwards failed to properly supervise M.

3. Respondent improperly by executed an option trade without securing the necessary documentation.

4. The above acts and omissions by the Respondent's constituted violations by the Respondents of 1) the Securities Act of 1933, 2) the Securities and Exchange Act of 1934 and 3) the Mississippi Securities Act.

111

Respondents denied all of the claims of the Claimant and further alleged the following defenses:

1. Failure to state a claim upon which relief can be granted since there is no private right of action under NASD and NYSE rules;

2. Claimant's claims are barred by her failure to object within 10 days of her receipt of the confirmations;

3. Estoppel, waiver, ratification and latches;

4. Failure of the Claimant to mitigate her damages;

5. Contributory negligence;

6. Assumption of the risk;

7. Claimant's damages were caused by unforeseeable market conditions; and

8. Statute of limitations.

RELIEF REQUESTED

Claimant requested damages equal to the following:

Margin interest in the amount of $20,000.00, commissions in the amount of $47,119.00, lost profits, pre-judgement interest, punitive damages in the amount of $1,000,000.00, attorney's fees and costs.

Respondents counterclaimed for their attorney's fees and costs and requested dismissal of the Claimant's claims.

AWARD

1. A. G. Edwards & Sons, Inc. and E. M. shall be jointly and severally liable for and shall pay to K. R. Three Thousand Six Hundred Sixteen Dollars and Ten Cents ($3,616.10).

2. The parties shall bear their own costs including attorneys' fees.

DATE AND PLACE

June 1 and 2, 1989; December 18 and 19, 1989; January 3, 1990 in New Orleans

NOTE: Suitability. Did not explain risks of margin accounts.

Number: 136MF

Claimant: L. W.

Respondents: Rauscher, Pierce Refnes, Inc. and Putman Financial Services, Inc.

CASE SUMMARY

In a claim filed with the NASD on February 1, 1988, Claimant L.W. ("Claimant") alleged that Respondent Rauscher Pierce Refnes, Inc. ("Rauscher") and Respondent Putman Financial Services, Inc. ("Putman") (collectively as "Respondents") failed to produce replacement certificates for his investment in Putman High Income Government Trust in a timely manner and that as a result incurred a loss in the amount of $109,166.33. In an Amendment to the Statement of Claim filed with the NASD on November 14, 1989, Claimant requested punitive damages against Respondent Rauscher.

In its answer filed with the NASD on April 26, 1988, Respondent Rauscher stated that it issued replacement certificates in a timely manner after its requirements were met. In its Response to the Amended Statement of Claim Respondent objected to the request for punitive damages.

In its answer filed with the NASD on February 24, 1989 Respondent Putman denies any liability for the alleged losses incurred by Claimant stating the losses were a result of his delay in returning the required documents.

AWARD

1. Rauscher Pierce Refnes, Inc. is liable for and shall pay to Claimant L. W. the

sum of Fifteen Thousand Dollars and no cents ($15,000.00);

2. Putman Financial Services, Inc. shall be and hereby is dismissed from the proceeding;

3. The parties shall bear each their own respective costs and fees including attorney's fees not specifically enumerated herein incurred in this proceeding.

DATE AND PLACE

February 12, 1990 in Houston, Texas

NOTE: Replace certificates in a timely manner.

Number: 137MF

Claimant: H. & K. M.

Respondents: Shearson Lehman Hutton, P. N. and C. S.

CASE SUMMARY

Dated filed: 6/14/88

First scheduled: 6/6/89

Decided: 6/6/89

Customers v. Member Firm and Registered Reps. for failure to following customers' instructions (CSs, Money Market or Ginney Maes) regarding investment of a lump sum pension payment. Respondents assert Claimants' overriding concern was growth rather than safety and consented to investment in "high yield" funds and that losses were due to "legitimate market fluctuations" and not by their actions.

<table>
<tr><th>RELIEF REQUESTED</th><th>AWARD</th></tr>
<tr><td>$12,067.71</td><td>Award: $2,500</td></tr>
<tr><td></td><td>Costs: $800.00</td></tr>
</table>

Respondent Shearson Lehman Hutton is hereby ordered to pay to the Claimants the sum of $2,500.00. Respondents are to be assessed the costs of $800.00 in this matter.

DATE AND PLACE

June 6, 1989 in Miami, Florida

NOTE: Failure to follow instructions on investment objectives.

115

Number: 138MF

Claimant: H. & M. E.

Respondents: Merrill Lynch, Pierce, Fenner & Smith, Inc.

CASE SUMMARY

Claimants allege that Respondent improperly recommended a swap between series of the Municipal Investment Trust Fund which resulted in a decrease in the monthly payout to Claimants.

RELIEF REQUESTED

$1,437.60

AWARD

Respondent is hereby ordered to pay to the Claimant the sum of $975.00; further, the costs, $25.00, which are payable to the New York Stock Exchange, Inc., are hereby assessed against the Respondent.

DATE AND PLACE

June 16, 1989 in New York City, New York

NOTE: Filed for arbitration for small amount.

Number: 139MF

Claimant: H. & J. K.

Respondents: Paine Webber, Inc. and T. T.

CASE SUMMARY

Claimants filed this action on June 13, 1988 against Respondents for negligence, failure to disclose material facts, and for the recommendation of unsuitable securities in light of Claimants investment objectives. Claimants invested a total of $200,000.00 in shares of the Franklin California Insured Tax Free Income Fund ("Franklin Fund") on February 4, 1987 and April 15, 1987 respectively, through respondents Paine Webber, Inc. and T. T. Claimants alleged that in making the investment recommendation to purchase the Franklin Fund, Respondent did not disclose that the principal amount invested in the Fund was subject to fluctuation in response to fluctuation in the interest rate. Additionally, Claimants alleged that Respondent T. acted in reckless and wanton disregard of Claimants' best interests and in breach of his fiduciary duty.

Respondents maintain that neither T. or Paine Webber, Inc. solicited the Claimants nor initially recommended that the Claimants purchase the Franklin Fund. Respondents further maintain that in accepting Claimants order for this purchase a suitable investment was made, that the Claimants were provided with all the information necessary to make an informed investment decision, that the losses realized by the Claimants were due to their choice to liquidate their investment in the Franklin Fund on October 19, 1987 against the advice of Respondent T., and that Claimants are solely responsible for bearing the consequences of adverse market conditions on the value of their investment. Additionally, Respondents raise the affirmative defenses of assumption of the risk, estoppel, authorization and/or ratification of all transactions, waiver, and that Respondents discharged its duties in good faith and

exercised the care, diligence and skill which ordinarily prudent men would
exercise in similar circumstances and like positions.

RELIEF REQUESTED

Claimants requested actual damages of $50,000.00, plus punitive damages in an
amount at least equal to the amount of actual damages award, interest from October
15, 1987 on the amounts awarded at money market rates, and attorneys' fees and
costs of this proceeding. Respondents requested dismissal of the claim in its
entirety, together with costs of this proceeding. Respondents further maintain that
the Statement of Claim fails to state a cause of action upon which exemplary or
punitive damages may be awarded and which attorneys' fees may be recovered.

AWARD

1. Respondents Paine Webber, Inc. and T. T. are hereby jointly and severally liable
for and shall pay to Claimants H. & J. K. the sum of Twenty Four Thousand, Sixty
Two Dollars and Zero Cents ($24,062.00).

2. The claim for punitive damages is hereby dismissed.

3. The claim for interest on the amount awarded is hereby dismissed.

4. The parties shall each bear their respective costs including attorneys' fees.

DATE AND PLACE

June 6, 1989 in Los Angeles, California

**NOTE: Misrepresented facts and failure to disclose fluxation in price of
fund.**

Number: 141MF

Claimant: M. R.

Respondent: Shearson Lehman Hutton, Inc.

CASE SUMMARY

Date filed: 4/25/89

First scheduled: 9/15/89

Decided: 9/15/89

Claimants allege an unauthorized liquidation of their mutual fund.

RELIEF REQUESTED

$11,441.00

AWARD

Award: $1,984.90   Costs: $400.00

Respondent shall pay to Claimant the sum of $2,384.90 on the claim, representing $1,984.90 as an award on the claim and $400.00 as a return of costs. In addition, Respondent is to pay $350.00 in interest.

DATE AND PLACE

September 15, 1989 in New York City, New York

NOTE: Unauthorized trading.

119

Number: 142MF

Claimant: T. L.

Respondents: Shearson Lehman Hutton and J. A.

CASE SUMMARY

Claimant T. L. alleged that Respondents Shearson Lehman Hutton and J. A. misinformed him with respect to a Government Trust offering he had invested in. Respondents maintain that Claimant possessed a copy of the Prospectus upon investing which clearly states that investors were admonished to carefully read the prospectus and retain it for future reference.

RELIEF REQUESTED

Claimant T. L. requested damages of $2,370.00. Respondents requested dismissal of claim and that Respondents be awarded costs and attorney's fees incurred in this matter.

AWARD

The Respondents are jointly and severally liable and shall pay the sum of Two Thousand Thirty Dollars and No Cents ($2,030.00) to the Claimant. The Respondents' request for costs and attorney's fees is hereby dismissed.

The parties shall each bear their respective costs including attorney's fees.

NOTE: **Misrepresentation.**

Number: 143MF

Claimant: J. D.

Respondents: A. G. Edwards & Sons, Inc. and B. S.

CASE SUMMARY

Claimant ("D") alleged that Respondents, A. G. Edwards & Sons, Inc. and Mr. B. S. failed to properly execute his order of October 15, 1987 to sell all of his mutual funds which were being held in four IRS Rollover Accounts and place the proceeds in money market accounts. Respondent alleged that on October 16, 1987 Davis authorized that all Davis investments would be transferred into Investment Portfolio, Inc.'s Money Market Fund. Respondents stated that Davis' instructions were transmitted to Portfolio's, Inc. the Claimant assumed the risk of investing the securities, and Davis' damages were caused by market factors beyond Respondents' control.

RELIEF REQUESTED

Davis' requested damages of $22,500.502 plus interest. Respondent requested the dismissal of all the Claimants claims.

AWARD

The panel awards damages of $22,500.52 plus interest of $2,400.00 to Davis

121

against Respondent A. G. Edwards & Sons, Inc. The claim against B. S. is hereby dismissed. Davis shall be refunded his $400.00 deposit by the NASD and Respondent A. G. Edwards & Sons, Inc. is assessed forum costs in the amount of $400.00 payable to NASD through its staff counsel. Each of the parties shall bear their respective costs including attorney's fees.

DATE AND PLACE

June 13, 1989 in Houston, Texas

NOTE: Failure to follow instructions.

Number: 144MF

Claimant: J. & M. B.

Respondent: Thomson McKinnon Securities, Inc.

CASE SUMMARY

In a claim filed with the NASD on July 26, 1988, Claimants J. & M. B. (Claimants) alleged that Claimants purchased from Respondent Thomson McKinnon Securities, Inc. (Thomson McKinnon) 95 units of National Municipal Trust Insurance Series 17 with a stated yield of 9.48% as set forth on the confirmation notice and monthly statement and as quoted to Claimant by a sales representative of Thomson McKinnon, Claimant further alleged that he read in the prospectus, which he received three weeks after his purchase, that the bond trust purchased from Thomson McKinnon was to yield 7.48% instead of 9.48%. Claimants alleged this was a breach of contract.

Thomson McKinnon maintained that the confirmation, monthly statement and quotation by the sales representative were erroneous. This bond trust offering was a prospectus offering. The terms, conditions and yields as disclosed in the prospectus were, therefore, the binding and accurate elements of the transaction. Since the stated yield of 9.48% was an error, there was no contract formed for lack of a "meeting of the minds" between the parties. As such, the damages sought by Claimants are excessive.

RELIEF REQUESTED

Claimants requested the difference between the price they paid to Thomson McKinnon for the stated yield of 9.48% and 7.48% as set forth the prospectus. This amount is $19,591.83, plus interest at the rate of 2% per annum of $92,705.75 from May 12, 1986 to date of payment. Claimants also requested assessment of the arbitration costs against Thomson McKinnon.

If any liability to Claimants was found by the arbitration panel, Thomson McKinnon requested that the appropriate remedy was the rescission of the alleged contract as being void ab initio and/or unconscionable, thereby allowing Thomson McKinnon to repurchase the 95 NMT Series 17 units for Claimants purchase price with Claimants to retain all interest earned to date and assessment of the arbitration fees equally against the parties.

AWARD

1. Claimants are entitled to rescind their purchase of 95 units of National Municipal Trust Insurance Series 17 (NMT-17). Accordingly, upon tender of the 95 units of (NMT-17) to Thomson McKinnon by the Claimants, Thomson McKinnon shall pay to the Claimants, jointly, the sum of Ninety-two Thousand Eight Hundred Ninety-eight Dollars and Sixty Cents ($92,898.60);

2. Thomson McKinnon is also liable for and shall pay to Claimants, interest on the principal amount Claimants invested with Thomson McKinnon at the rate of 2% annum from and inclusive of May 12, 1986 to and inclusive of May 12, 1987;

3. The Claimants' claim for damages in the amount of $19,591.83 shall be and is hereby dismissed in its entirety;

4. The Claimants' claim for interest at an annual rate of 7% payable on the sum invested with Thomson McKinnon shall be and is hereby dismissed in its entirety;

5. The parties shall each bear their respective costs and expenses including any attorney's fees incurred in this matter.

DATE AND PLACE

June 8, 1989 in Chicago, Illinois

NOTE: Cancelled trade since interest rate was misquoted.

Number: 145MF

Claimants: J. & A. Geracos

Respondent: Smith Barney

CASE SUMMARY

Date filed: 3/8/89

First scheduled: 3/17/89

Decided: 9/29/89

Customers vs. member firm for unauthorized trading of Putnam High Income Government Treasury Shares.

RELIEF REQUESTED

$6,011.11

AWARD

Respondent shall pay to the Claimant $6,011.11 plus interest payable at the rate of 8.5% from the date of the claim to the date of the award and thereafter at the New York State legal rate until actually paid to the Claimant. The Claimant shall surrender ownership of 543 shares or Putnam High Income Government Trust Fund. Costs are assessed against Smith Barney, et al.

DATE AND PLACE

September 29, 1989 in New York City, New York

Number: 147MF

Claimant: J. G.

Respondents: Merrill Lynch, Pierce, Fenner & Smith, Inc. and R. K.

CASE SUMMARY

J. G. ("Claimant") alleged as follows:

1.   Merrill Lynch, Pierce, Fenner & Smith, Inc. and R. K. ("Respondents") misrepresented the commission arrangements regarding the American Cap Comstock Fund and Delcap Fund in the months of May and September respectively of 1987.

2. Respondents failed to properly execute Claimants order of August 31, 1987 to sell all positions in Delaware and Delcap Funds and place the proceeds in Respondents' cash management account.

3. Respondents failed to properly execute the Claimants order to purchase shares in Government Bond Funds instead purchasing shares in the Delchester Bond Fund.

4. The above acts constituted violations of federal and state securities laws. Respondents denied each and every claim of the Claimant.

RELIEF REQUESTED

Claimant requested damages of $48,932.28 plus costs and attorney's fees.

Respondent requested that all of the Claimant's claims be dismissed with prejudice and an award from the Claimant for its cost and attorney's fees.

AWARD

1. Respondents Merrill Lynch and R. K. are jointly and severally liable to and shall pay to the Claimant J. G. $14,454.00;

2. The parties shall bear their own respective costs and attorney's fees.

DATE AND PLACE

August 23, 1989

NOTE: Misrepresented commissions and failed to follow instructions.

Number: 148MF

Claimants: C. & G. G.

Respondents: Dean Witter Reynolds, Inc. and L. G.

CASE SUMMARY

This claim was filed with the NASD, Inc. on August 29, 1988. The hearing was conducted in Tampa, Florida on September 20, 1989 with a total of 2 sessions.

Claimants, C. & G. G. ("the G's") alleged that Respondents, Dean Witter Reynolds, Inc. ("Dean Witter") and L. G. ("G") were liable for misrepresentation and for failing to inform them of all the risks associated with the investments that Claimants were placed in. Specifically, Claimants alleged that G's misstatements as to the expected rate of return induced Claimants to purchase Dean Witter's U.S. Government Trust, which investment was not consistent with Claimants' stated investment objectives. Respondents alleged that Claimants were informed of all the risks because they were given a prospectus and that Respondents made no misstatements and made complete and accurate disclosure of all material facts.

RELIEF REQUESTED

Claimants requested damages in the amount of Fifteen Thousand Nine Hundred Fifty-Eight and 00/100 ($15,958.00) Dollars. Respondents requested dismissal of the claim, attorney's fees and other costs.

AWARD

1. Respondent, Dean Witter, is hereby liable and shall pay to Claimants the amount of Four Thousand Six Hundred and 00/100 ($4,600.00) Dollars as compensatory damages for their own account.

2. Respondent, G., is not liable and, therefore, all claims against him are hereby dismissed.

3. Respondents' request for attorney's fees is hereby dismissed in all respects.

DATE AND PLACE

September 20, 1989

NOTE: Misrepresented risks.

Number: 150MF

Claimant: R. H.

Respondents: Kidder Peabody & Co. and W. C.

CASE SUMMARY

Date filed: 8/19/89

First scheduled: 4/20/89

Customer v. Member Firm and Registered Representative - Claimant alleges that Respondent broker induced him to liquidate his portfolio of Putnam & Kemper Option Funds to invest in "Oil & Gas Trust" in a margin account. Claimant further alleges to be an unsophisticated investor. The advice given was unsuitable and inconsistent with the stated account objectives and prior course of dealing.

AWARD

The Claimant is to be awarded $5,000.00 and all costs are to be divided equally.

DATE AND PLACE

November 3, 1989 in Philadelphia, Pennsylvania

NOTE: Important: broker's advise was inconsistent with the stated account objectives and prior course of dealings.

Number: 151MF

Claimant: D. B.

Respondent: PaineWebber, Inc.

CASE SUMMARY

This proceeding was commenced by the Claimant D. B. against the Respondent PaineWebber, Inc. arising from certain transactions in the Claimant's account during the period of 1985 to 1987. Ms. B. alleged that the Respondent PaineWebber, Inc. through its broker S. D. recommended the purchase of an investment which was unsuitable for her account. Specifically, Claimant asserts that the broker recommended the liquidation of her investment in American Capital Government Securities, Inc., and the subsequent purchase of Decatur II Series Fund, an investment unsuitable for her account.

Respondent PaineWebber, Inc. denies the allegations of the Claimant. Respondent contends that Claimant was knowledgeable of the transactions in the account and assumed the risks inherent in the purchase of the fund.

RELIEF REQUESTED

Claimant requests damages in excess of $25,494.13, plus interest, costs and attorney's fees. Respondent requests a dismissal of the claim in its entirety.

131

AWARD

1. Respondent PaineWebber, Inc. shall be liable and shall pay to Claimant D. B. the sum of Eleven Thousand Five Hundred Dollars and No Cents ($11,500.00).

2. The parties shall each bear their respective costs including attorney's fees.

DATE

September 13, 1989

NOTE: Investment occurred 2-4 years prior to arbitration award. Suitability.

Number: 152MF

Claimant: S.C. & B.M.I.

Respondent: KMS Financial Services, Inc.

J.E.H. and J.R.H.

CASE SUMMARY

This case was filed with the National Association of Securities Dealers Inc. ("NASD") on September 13, 1988. Claimants alleged the following: failure to execute sale and purchase order for mutual funds.

Respondent KMS Financial Services, Inc. ("KMS") denied the failure to properly execute the trade according to its terms and alleged the following affirmative defenses: contributory negligence and erroneous calculation of alleged damages. KMS asserted a cross-claim against Respondents J.E.H. and J.R.H. for contribution and indemnification for any award assessed against KMS.

Respondents J.R.H. and J.E.H. denied each and every substantive allegation of Claimants and Cross-Claimants.

RELIEF REQUESTED

Claimant requested: 1) compensatory damages of $35,000.00; 2) interest at 12% per annum from October 7, 1987 to the date of award; and 3) attorneys fees and costs.

AWARD

1.   Respondent KMS Financial Services, Inc., only, is liable for and shall pay to Claimants the sum of $17,280.71, which includes an award of interest.

2.   Each and every claim against Respondent J.R.H. and J.E.H. is dismissed.

3.   The cross-claims of KMS Financial Services, Inc. against Cross-Respondents J.R.H. and J.E.H. are dismissed.

4.   The parties shall each bear their respective costs including attorney's fees.

DATE AND PLACE

May 30, 1990 in Seattle, Washington

NOTE: Failure to follow instructions.

CHAPTER 10

STOCKS AND OPTIONS - ARBITRATION AWARD

Number: 301SO

Claimant: KMK

Respondents: CTW, Merrill Lynch, Pierce, Fenner and Smith

CASE SUMMARY

In a claim filed with the NASD on September 15, 1987, Claimants alleged that Respondents Merrill Lynch Pierce Fenner & Smith and CTW purchased speculative and unsuitable LTV Corp. cumulative convertible Preferred Stock for KMK's IRA accounts and Entex Energy Development for the KMK's joint account.

Merrill Lynch and CTW denied the allegations of the claim and asserted various affirmative defenses including but not limited to estoppel, ratification, contributory negligence and failure to mitigate damages.

RELIEF REQUESTED

KMK requested damages of $12,500 plus a gain on that money calculated with respect to the Standard & Poor's 500 index.

Merrill Lynch and CTW requested dismissal of the claim and that the costs of the proceeding be assessed against KMK.

AWARD

The arbitration panel, having considered the pleadings, the testimony, and the evidence presented at the hearing, has decided in full and final resolution of the issues submitted for determination as follows:

1. The Respondents Merrill Lynch and CTW are liable for and shall pay to KMK, jointly, the total sum of Eight Thousand Two Hundred Ninety-Six Dollars and Sixty-Nine Cents ($8,296.69) which sum is apportioned as follows;

    a. Merrill Lynch is liable for and shall pay to KMK, jointly the sum of Four Thousand Nine Hundred Seventy-Eight Dollars and One Cent ($4,978.01);

    b. CTW is liable for and shall pay to KMK, jointly the sum of Three Thousand Eight Hundred Eighteen Dollars and Sixty-Eight Cents ($3,318.68).

DATE AND PLACE

October 5 and 6, 1989 in St. Louis, Missouri.

NOTE: Suitability. Broker was personally liable.

Number: 302SO

Claimant: JKC

Respondents: First Affiliated Securities, Inc. and TG

SUMMARY OF ISSUES

This case was filed on December 9, 1987. Claimant JKC alleges that Respondents First Affiliated Securities, Inc. and TG made unsuitable investments in her account, such as, limited partnerships, speculative securities and options with the use of margin. Said investments were allegedly made without regard to Claimants objectives which were income generation and safety of principal.

Respondents allege that Claimant had investment experience and all trades in her account were either at her direction or with her consent and knowledge.

DAMAGES AND RELIEF REQUESTED

Claimants seek general damages according to proof; interest on said sum; punitive damages; costs and attorneys' fees.

Respondents seek dismissal of the claim in its entirety.

DAMAGES AND RELIEF AWARDED

1. First Affiliated Securities, Inc. and TG are jointly and severally liable and shall pay to Claimant the principal sum of Fifty-One Thousand Two Hundred Dollars and No Cents ($51,200.00) and interest there on at the rate of 8% annum from April 23, 1986, until paid in full.

2. Respondent TG is solely liable and shall pay to claimant the sum of Eight Thousand, Eight Hundred Dollars and No Cents ($8,800.00) plus interest thereon at the rate of 8% per annum from April 23, 1986 until paid in full.

3. Respondent First Affiliated Securities, Inc. is solely liable and shall pay to Claimant the sum of Twenty Thousand Dollars and No Cents ($20,000.00) plus interest thereon at the rate of 8% per annum from April 23, 1986 until paid in full.

DATE AND PLACE

October 11 and 18, 1989 in Los Angeles, California.

NOTE: Suitability. Broker was personally liable.

Number: 303SO

Claimant: GO

Respondents: Graystone Nash, Inc., SB and DW

CASE SUMMARY

This claim was filed with the NASD, Inc. on February 24, 1988. The hearing was conducted in Ft. Lauderdale, Florida on February 12, 1990 with a total of two sessions.

Claimant, GO, alleged that Respondents, Graystone Nash, Inc. ("Graystone"), SB, and DW, failed to execute sell orders of his entire portfolio of common stocks at the bid price on October 27, 1987 or at all; that Respondents sold certain of his securities at prices less than the authorized prices; that Respondents were negligent; breached their contract with Claimant; and, violated Section 517.301, Florida Statutes.

Graystone denied all allegations of wrongdoing; alleged that no contract for same day execution was made with Claimant; that Claimant was aware of the turbulent market conditions and that all prices were subject to change; and, that all executions would be made at market price. Graystone cross claimed against SB for indemnification.

RELIEF REQUESTED

Claimant requested compensatory damages in the amount of $17,568.75; interest at the legal rate from October 27, 1987 in the amount of $4,831.41, for a total of $22,400.16; punitive damages; attorney's fees; costs; and, damages pursuant to Sections 517.211 and 517.241, Florida Statutes.

AWARD

Respondents, Graystone, SB, and DW, are hereby liable, jointly and severally, and shall pay to the Claimant the amount of Seventeen Thousand Five Hundred Sixty Eight and 75/100 ($17,568.75) Dollars, plus interest at the legal rate of 12% per annum from October 27, 1987 in the amount of Four Thousand Eight Hundred Thirty One and 41/100 ($4,831.41) Dollars, for a total due to Claimant of Twenty Two Thousand Four Hundred and 16/100 ($22,400.16) Dollars.

NOTE: Negligence.

Number: 304SO

Claimant: FDF

Respondents: PaineWebber, Inc., RD and FOB

CASE SUMMARY

Claimant FD alleged that Respondents PaineWebber, Inc. ("PaineWebber"), RD, and FOD, were liable for: misrepresentation; churning; violations of Federal and Florida Securities Laws; breach of fiduciary duty; fraud and negligence, either directly or under the theory of Respondent superior. Additionally, Claimant alleged that PaineWebber and FOB were liable for negligent supervision.

Respondents alleged that FOB was advised of all the risks; made the decision to exercise his employee stock options and invest in speculative stocks; was suitable for the trading he engaged in and authorized all transactions. Respondents asserted the affirmative defenses of waiver; estoppel; failure to mitigate damages; comparitive negligence; negligence; failure to rely on the statements or omissions; lack of proximate cause; assumption of risk and statute of limitations.

RELIEF REQUESTED

Claimant requested damages in the amount of $85,061.64 plus interest, punitive damages, attorney's fees and other costs. Respondents requested dismissal of the claim.

AWARD

Respondents PaineWebber, RD, and FOB are hereby liable, jointly and severally, and shall pay to the Claimant the amount of Sixty Three Thousand Seven Hundred Ninety Six and 23/100 ($63,796.23) Dollars inclusive of interest at the legal rate of 12% per annum.

DATE AND PLACE

September 9th and 19th in Ft. Lauderdale, Florida.

NOTE: Misrepresentation, churning, and negligence.

Number: 305SO

Claimant: HR

Respondents: Dean Witter Reynolds, Inc. and AO

CASE SUMMARY

This claim was filed on August 29, 1988 and amended February 23, 1989 and October 23, 1989. The claim originally named SEJ as a respondent but his bankruptcy filing resulted in an automatic stay of the proceeding as to him. The Claimant alleged that Dean Witter Reynolds, Inc. acting by and through its account executive SEJ, engaged in unauthorized and excessive trading in his account. The Claimant further alleged that Respondents induced him to enter into margin activity and trading in uncovered put and call options, which were unsuitable for him, without adequately explaining the risks involved therein.

The Claimant stated that SEJ solicited the Claimant to purchase interests in 2 limited partnerships through false and misleading statements as to the quality and nature of said investments. The Claimant also stated that Dean Witter Reynolds, Inc. and AO failed to properly supervise the activities of SEJ.

Respondents Dean Witter Reynolds, Inc. and AO alleged that JH was a knowledgeable, experienced, and sophisticated person and investor. They further alleged the claimant was in control of all trading done in his account and that Respondents made full and fair disclosures of the potential risks of making certain investments.

144

Respondents stated that the investments made were consistent with the Claimant's objectives and that no misrepresentations or misstatements were made to the Claimant.

RELIEF REQUESTED

The Claimant asked for the recovery of $545,246.00 plus treble damages, punitive damages, prejudgment and post judgment interest, attorney fees, expert witness fees and costs.

The Respondents asked that the claims be denied and that they recover their costs.

AWARD

Respondents Dean Witter Reynolds, Inc. and AO are hereby jointly and severally liable for and shall pay to the Claimant the sum of Two Hundred Ten Thousand Dollars, in case, inclusive of interest.

NOTE: Unauthorized trading, negligence, suitability. Dean Witter Reynolds said JH was a knowledgeable, experienced person and investor.

Number: 306SO

Claimant: LM

Respondent: Shearson Lehman Hutton, Inc.

CASE SUMMARY

Claimant alleges that Respondent ignored his specific instructions and put 10,000 shares of Farmers' Group, Inc. into his account pursuant to put options which Claimant alleges were back-timed or backdated. As a result of Respondent's action, Claimant alleges that the 10,000 shares were put to him improperly at $60 per share and that he could have purchased the same in the open market at 55 1/8 per share.

Respondent denies the allegations of wrongdoing and further alleges that Claimant sustained no damages.

RELIEF REQUESTED

Claimant requests that the panel award him $50,000, interest, commissions paid and attorney's fees. Respondent requests that the panel dismiss the claim and award it attorney's fees.

AWARD

Respondent is hereby liable to the Claimant in the amount of Three Thousand, Eight Hundred Dollars and Zero Cents ($3,800.00)

PLACE

New York, New York

Number: 307SO

Claimant: NC

Respondent: Merrill Lynch, Pierce, Fenner & Smith, Inc.

CASE SUMMARY

Claimant NC alleged that Respondent Merrill Lynch, Pierce, Fenner & Smith, Inc. failed to execute orders to sell common stock on October 19, 1987, misrepresented the amount of commission discounts that he would receive and allegedly inflicted emotional distress on the Claimant by their actions.

Respondents maintained that pandemonium reigned on the stock market on October 19, 1989 and Merrill Lynch performed well in executing some of the sell orders of Claimant on that day. Merrill Lynch further denied that it misrepresented the amount of commission discount the Claimant was to receive for his account.

RELIEF REQUESTED

Claimant NC requested relief in the amount of $16,640.00 plus interest, costs and attorneys fees. Respondent Merrill Lynch, Pierce, Fenner & Smith, Inc. requested that the claim of the Claimant be dismissed plus costs of its defense.

AWARD

Respondent Merrill Lynch, Pierce, Fenner & Smith, Inc. is liable and shall pay to the Claimant NC the sum of Four Thousand Seventy Four Dollars and Twenty One Cents ($4,074.21).

PLACE: Boston, Massachusetts

Number: 308SO

Claimant: R & MY

Respondents: EF Hutton & Co., Inc., RK and PW

SUMMARY OF ISSUES

This case was filed on July 19, 1989. Claimants alleged that Respondents engaged in unauthorized stock transactions, and option transactions, placed Claimants in unsuitable investments.

DAMAGES AND RELIEF REQUESTED

Claimants requested an award of $31,854.48 plus at least $63,308.00 in punitive damages, together with the cost incurred in this action.

DAMAGES AND RELIEF AWARDED

Respondent RK is liable for and shall pay to Claimants the sum of Five Thousand Dollars and No Cents ($5,000.00). Said liability is individual liability.
Respondent EF Hutton & Co., Inc. (now Shearson Lehman Hutton, Inc.) is liable for and shall pay to claimants the sum of Five Thousand Dollars and No Cents ($5,000). Said liability is sole liability.

NOTE: Suitability unauthorized trading. Broker held personally liable.

148

Number: 309SO

Claimant: JW

Respondents: JW Charles Securities, Inc. f/k/a JW Charles Bush Securities, Inc. and JA

CASE SUMMARY

Claimant JW alleged that Respondent JW Charles Securities, Inc. ("J.W.C.") was negligent in the handling of instituting stop loss orders and the cancellations of such stop orders in Home Shopping Network stock; that their procedures for processing such orders were inadequate; and, that their negligence caused a loss to Claimant. Respondent alleged that it properly handled all stop loss orders, was not negligent and that any losses were the result of market conditions.

RELIEF REQUESTED

Claimant requested damages of $15,026.50, plus interest from March 19, 1987. Respondent requested dismissal of the claim and costs assessed against Claimant.

AWARD

Respondent J.W.C. is hereby liable and shall pay to Claimant the amount of Seven Thousand and 00/100 ($7,000.00) Dollars, inclusive of interest.

CHAPTER 11

WERE YOU CAUGHT UP IN TECHNOLOGY OR THE INTERNET BOOM?

Update 2002

These stocks and funds were hot from 1996 to 1999. Most mutual fund families jumped on the bandwagon and created these funds and generated tens of millions in management and other fees. When the bubble burst and these stocks and funds began to fall in April 2000 billions of dollars in NAV evaporated over the next two years. Some funds are down from their high as much as 80%. Many of the companies are now gone. Many of the mutual funds raised money from investors based on the fund's performance and appreciation. Some brokers and brokerage firms didn't consider if the clients were suitable for these investments.

Arbitration cases on these investments have now been filed and are now beginning the arbitration process. I've listed a few cases below to give you an idea of the types of cases that are now being filed.

If clients were unsuitable for these investments, many brokerage firms will pay back part or all of the investor's losses. If you believe your are one of these investors call or email me and I will review your potential case.

Arbitration Cases

01-###34 March 2002
Claimant vs. Dreyfus Brokerage Services
Case Summary: Claimant alleged trading system flaws in purchasing stock via the Internet
through Dreyfus Brokerage Services Online system. Claimant awarded $19,196.56.
This amount represented 100% of the claim.

01-###93 January 2002
Claimants vs. Auerbach, Pollack, & Richardson
Case Summary: Unauthorized purchases of
Internet Capital Group. Claimants award:
$28,908.00 & $36,691.80 in compensatory damages.
**These amounts represented 100% of the
requested amounts.**

#01-###42 January 2002
Claimant vs. Merrill Lynch
Case Summary: Negligence, Breach of contract,
and other allegations involving transactions of
PurchasePro.com, Inc.
Claimant award: Merrill Lynch shall provide
claimants with 2,000 shares of
PurchasePro.com and is liable and shall pay the
claimants $99,000.00. **Claimants requested
$100,000.00 in compensatory damages.**

#01-###46   October 2001
Claimant vs E*Trade Securities, Inc.
Case Summary: Claimant alleged the respon-
dent made an unauthorized sell order causing a
loss to his account.
Claimant award: $10,938.00.
**Claimant received 100% of his claim plus
$4,375.00 in attorney fees.**

#00-###95   January 2001
Claimants vs. Neuberger Berman and others
Case Summary: Alleged causes of action from
unauthorized trading, Misrepresentations,
Failure to Disclose, unsuitability, and many others.
Claimant award: In excess of $103,000.00.
One of the defenses respondent tried to use
was " market conditions beyond the control of
respondents"

#01-###92   February 2002
Claimant vs E*Trade Securities
Case Summary: Claimant asserted Breach of
contract, conversion, fraud, and other causes of
action involving the stock and options of
Technology Solutions Company and the stock of
eLoyalty Corp.
Claimant Award: $191,000.00

\#00-###77   October 2001
Claimants vs. Marion Bass Securities Corp plus nine other respondents.
Case Summary: Claimant asserts churning and securities fraud, breach of fiduciary duty, plus other causes of action.
Claimant award: **In addition to actual damages, claimant received punitive damages.**

CHAPTER 12

MEDIATION: TAKE CONTROL OVER THE OUTCOME OF YOUR DISPUTE

Update 2002

When I first became an arbitrator for the NASD in February 1992 arbitration was the main avenue to resolve disputes. A few years earlier the NASD tried a pilot program with the American Arbitration Association and U.S. Arbitration and Mediation, Inc to have the parties consider mediation as an alternative to arbitration. The main reason for the NASD was simple. Most cases settle prior to the arbitrators making a final decision. Why go through the time and expense if you're open to settlement. This would be an enormous benefit to both parties. Over the past ten years mediation has become the resolution process of choice before arbitration.

Since the bear market began in April 2000 more complaints have been filed with the NASD.This means more people are open to all means to resolve their dispute. As people contact the

NASD for information about filing a complaint, mediation is suggested as an alternative or beginning before arbitration. They are told that filing for arbitration doesn't negate there proceeding with mediation first; or that beginning with mediation doesn't hurt them in arbitration. In fact filing for arbitration and notifying the respondents you're wanting to mediate before arbitrate shows your willingness to quickly resolve the dispute.

As a mediator and arbitrator for the NASD, I've found all cases filed for arbitration also qualify for mediation. The most common complaints in order of controversies that are filed and suited for both mediation and arbitration are:
- Breach of Fiduciary Duty
- Negligence
- Failure to Supervise
- Misrepresentation
- Unsuitability
- Unauthorized Trading
- Omission of Facts
- Churning

Compare Mediation and Arbitration

When we talk about mediation verses arbitration it's not an either/or situation. If both parties cannot come to a voluntary compromise in mediation then arbitration would be used in resolving the dispute.

The initial benefits in resolving a dispute in mediation compared to arbitration is time and money. Here are some quick facts:

1. The time line of an agreement to mediate to resolving the dispute in mediation is usually 60-120 days compared to one year or longer for arbitration. In fact, if a mediator is available and both parties agree a mediation can be done within days of an agreement to mediate.
2. Disputes are usually resolved in mediation within one session. This is usually between four and eight hours using one mediator. It is common for an arbitration to take three days with a panel of three arbitrators.
3. Mediations don't require an attorney, witnesses, experts, or volumes of documents to persuade the brokerage firm to come to an agreement. That could be a saving of thousands of dollars. To prove your case in arbitration these expenses are usually required by both claimant and respondent. $10,000.00 to $20,000.00 in expenses for each side is not uncommon. In arbitration I strongly recommended that a securities attorney represent a claimant.
4. An experienced mediator has an hourly rate of $150.00 - $300.00 that is split between both parties. In an average session of six hours with the mediator getting $250.00 an hour the total cost

for the mediator would be $1,500.00. Each side would be responsible for $750.00. In addition the claimant will pay a mediation-filling fee which could be $50.00 - $300.00 depending on the amount in dispute and the brokerage firms mediation filing fees range from $150.00-$500.00. In arbitration each side is responsible for their own costs. Attorney's fees, expert witness fees, and arbitration panel fees for usually a three-day session. Preparation of documents (usually six copies of each document. One for each party, one for the NASD, and three for the arbitration panel). These are the hard costs. The intangible costs are more difficult to calculate such as interruption of personal and business life, loss of production, and the cost of emotion and stress for the preparation and duration of the arbitration.

5. A specific type of mediation that has gained in popularity is the telephonic mediation. This simply is mediation conducted by all parties by telephone. The major benefit is the savings of time and money. The claimants can be in one city with their attorney in another. The respondents, usually the broker and his manager, can be in their office and still be available to do business or answer questions for their other clients. Their attorney can be in another city. No traveling time or cost to fly everyone to one location. If the broker needs any documents he usually has them in his office. As long as each party has a fax

machine if documents are needed they can be faxed to all parties.

Other differences between mediation and arbitration are the following:

• Mediation is a voluntary collaborative problem solving process. Both parties must agree to any decisions or compromises that are made. Arbitration is an adversarial process where the arbitrators make all decisions. The parties are powerless in deciding the outcome of the dispute.

• Mediator does not make any decisions. He has no power over either party. He is there as a neutral to help facilitate a negotiated settlement (help both sides come to an acceptable compromise). Arbitrators are also neutral but are empowered by the parties to favor one side over the other for the purpose of determining the outcome of the dispute (based on the facts and evidence of the case).

• Mediation is a negotiation. Mediators try to show both parties their strengths and weaknesses of their case. The mediator helps the parties define and understand the interests of the other side. Arbitrators don't care about anything except the parties' position and the evidence, which supports their respective case. The parties' interests in the matter are not as important as their ability to prove their case. Arbitrators will render a decision based on the parties respective presentation of their case.

• In mediation the exchange of documents and information is limited. Usually one party will show the other only documents that will strengthen their case in the hope to accelerate a settlement. In an arbitration extensive exchange of all documents pertaining to the case is usually required. No stone is left unturned.

• In mediation all parties can say whatever they want anytime they want. It is an informal discussion between both sides. Each side can give suggestions and ideas if they feel it will help resolve the dispute. In arbitration the parties just present the facts. Usually the attorneys do all the speaking to the arbitrators. It is formal and each party is required to testify under oath.

• As a mediator I find the most positive part of the mediation is the ability to speak to both sides privately, without the other side being in the discussion. This is called a private session or caucus. This gives each side the ability to "let their hair down" and say exactly what is on their mind. They can vent, yell and scream and say exactly how they feel about the other side. They also tell the mediator their concerns and what they are really looking for. The mediator can also tell the party his concerns about the case based on the facts from the other side. All private sessions are private and confidential. The mediator cannot, unless he is given authorization to do so, mention any part of that private session. At the end of each private secession the mediator has a monetary offer or counter offer to give to the other side. In arbitration there is no private communications with the arbitrators.

• In mediation the outcome is based on the interests and needs of each party. If an agreement is made then it was mutually acceptable by each side. In arbitration any decision will make at least one side unhappy. I've seen arbitrations where both sides were unhappy with the decision.

The Actual Mediation

Before the mediation begins both sides should have sent me confidential information about their side of the case. Statement of claims, specific documents, plus a brief review of what they hope to accomplish at the mediation. By having the facts and reviewing each sides position, I'm able to understand and control the direction of the mediation.

The mediation begins when the mediator calls everyone into the room. The room is usually a conference room with a large table and chairs. Each party sits on their respective side. The mediator is usually at the head of the table at this time. When I'm the mediator I begin by trying to put all parties at ease. Usually the claimant is nervous since this is their first time at mediation. The brokerage firms representatives are usually used to the process. I begin by introducing myself and having all the parties introduce themselves. I ask both sides for permission if they mind if I speak to them by their first name. This tactic puts them more at ease.

Next I explain mediation and how the process works. I look at both sides equally as I explain it. This tactic makes both sides feel comfortable. One side isn't being treated better then the other. I thank both parties for choosing mediation and say it shows both parties willingness to try to settle this matter. I state mediation has a success settlement rate of over 80% so far in 2002. I explain that both sides will have an opening statement and that after the statements I will begin by speaking to each side privately. Each party at any time can say whatever they want. I am here as a neutral. Nether party has to accept any dollar amount offered by the other side. Understand that as a mediator I will do almost anything, whatever each party wants if it helps to resolve the dispute with a successful settlement. At the end of the opening statements I ask if anyone has anything else to say at this time before we begin. Everyone usually says no. I then make one last statement that concerns both sides. I say, **"after reviewing the information both sides gave me and if I was an arbitrator on this case and had to make a decision based on this information I promise you one side would not be happy with my decision"**. This is a true statement, In all the cases that I've mediated one side always had a stronger case then the other. This statement usually encourages both sides to compromise a little more since they are uncertain of how strong their case is. After that I begin the private sessions. I usually ask the respondents to go to another room and begin the private sessions with the claimant.

Negotiation from Strength in a Mediation

If both sides agree to mediate the dispute you must begin to gather as much information as you can to prove your case. Begin by collecting all your confirmations and statements. Try to remember all conversations and gather any additional documents.

As I stated in my book **'WHAT YOUR STOCK-BROKER DOESN'T WANT YOU TO KNOW'** the type of documents that can help you in arbitration can help you negotiate from strength in mediation. Here are some examples:

• If your account form states your investment objective is income and safety of principal and the broker bought you technology or internet stocks or mutual funds it's possible the broker breached his fiduciary duty and also you might be unsuitable for the investment. Show the other side your account form.

• If your account form states you have a liquid net worth of $100,000.00 and the broker brought 40%of your net worth of a sector mutual fund, the broker might have breached his fiduciary duty and you might be unsuitable for the investment. Show the other side your account form

• Any hand written memos from the broker stating why the investment would be good for you. Show the other side the note.

• Any articles from any publications showing your investment has more risk or is more aggressive than what your account form states you should be invested in. Show the other side the articles.

These are just a few examples on how you can deal from strength in mediation.

CHAPTER 13

COLUMNS AND ENDORSEMENTS

THE WALL STREET JOURNAL

MONEY & INVESTING

" Your Money Matters" – Ellen E. Schultz   October 29,1991

When It's the Wrong Time for Big Financial Decisions

…"An ambitious broker will contact the company and try to give a seminar to people who are laid off," says Bruce Sankin, a Fort Lauderdale, Florida financial consultant. "There's nothing wrong with that," he notes, people who have been laid off "need financial advice."…

July 9th, 1991

THE WALL STREET JOURNAL

MONEY & INVESTMENT

More Brokers Strike Out And Go Solo on the Street

By MICHAEL SICONOLFI
Staff Reporter of THE WALL STREET JOURNAL

NEW YORK — After seven years at Dean Witter Reynolds Inc. and Prudential Securities Inc., broker Bruce Sankin got the itch.

Tired of pressure to push the "product of the month," Mr. Sankin says, he struck out on his own this year and opened his own one-man brokerage firm in Plantation, Fla.

Working solo can cut the conflicts many big-firm brokers face, he says. "There's no, 'You've got to sell $10,000 of this stuff.' " the 44-year-old Mr. Sankin says from his bedroom office. The drawbacks: fatter medical and phone bills and nobody to keep him company except research reports.

Mr. Sankin, the Florida broker, says: "I don't touch limited partnerships; I don't do options; I rarely do stocks." Instead, he says he focuses on bonds and mutual funds.

June 1992

Money MAGAZINE

INVESTING

LENDING TO CUSTOMERS

Brokerage firms often let customers leverage their money by buying securities on margin. Typically, the customer puts up half the purchase price in cash and borrows the rest from the brokerage. Firms have two powerful incentives for encouraging margin buying. For one, it's profitable. Today, brokerages generally charge customers as much as 9% for margin loans, 1½ to 2¾ percentage points more than the firm pays to borrow the money from banks. Second, margin lending enables clients to buy twice as many securities. "That means double commissions for the firm," says Bruce Sankin, a former Prudential broker in Fort Lauderdale and author of *What Your Stockbroker Doesn't Want You to Know!* (Business Publishing, $22). But it also means twice the risk for margin investors: If you crap out on a margin account, not only have you lost your money, you've lost somebody else's as well—and you still have to pay interest on it.

WHAT YOUR STOCKBROKER DOESN'T WANT YOU TO KNOW!

Bruce Sankin, an investment counselor, the author of <u>What Your Stockbroker Doesn't Want You to Know</u>, ove the many years in his practice has learned that what a client says he wants and the risk he is willing to accep is, in reality, different than what he needs to achieve his financial goals. If you would like a financial plan o an analysis of your holdings, contact Mr. Sankin to review your financial goals and his services:

BRUCE N. SANKIN
c/o Business Publishing
P.O. Box 77-0001
Coral Springs, Florida 33077
(305) 346-8585

American Association of Individual Investors

AAII JOURNAL

July 1991   Volume XIII, Number 6

BRUCE SANKIN   COLUMNIST
SUN SENTINEL   WEEKLY BUSINESS   Fort Lauderdale

ARBITRATION

Some investor loss can be recovered

BRUCE SANKIN

Know the rules in pressing claims against brokerage firms

Timing important when filing claim for arbitration

Switching bond fund involves commission

Failure to give advice on risk leads to award

Giving prospectus to investor doesn't let broker off hook

Recourse possible in partnership loss

Class actions can limit investors future rights

The Brokerage Account Form: Handle With Care

By Bruce Sankin

Stockbrokers, in general, deal honestly and with integrity with their clients. But you should always understand that they are in business to make money. The more you understand about commission brokerage houses, the better value you can get for your money when dealing with them.

One aspect of dealing with brokerage houses that is often misunderstood by individual investors is the seemingly innocuous account form.

The account form is filled out either by you or your broker when you first open an account with a firm. In fact, everyone must have a completed account form to receive an account number. This is mandatory before a transaction between you and your stockbroker can oc-

and meaningless. It is at this point that the account form becomes vital in your defense at arbitration. Many of the disputes that wind up in arbitration focus on the individual's investment knowledge, and the account form is one of the first documents that a brokerage firm will turn to when such a dispute occurs.

Filling Out the Form

The client account form might look like a basic questionnaire with simple questions, but it is the document that shows if you are suited for certain types of investments. Do not answer these questions lightly or inaccurately, because it could cost you in the future.

Sun-Sentinel
June 17, 1991
COVER STORY

Pay close attention to brokerage account forms author says.

Financial adviser Bruce Sankin of Coral Springs displays his book he wrote to inform investors.

Do you own or rent your home? Do you own 10 percent or more of a business? How did you come to choose this brokerage firm to open your account?

They all seem like innocuous questions, just one more piece of paperwork in the annoying routine of opening a brokerage account. Yet investors' failure to fill out brokerage account forms themselves or their tendency to fill them out inaccurately can cost them dearly should a dispute arise with their broker, said Bruce Sankin, a broker who has recently written a book entitled *What Your Stockbroker Doesn't Want You To Know.*

BUSINESS

Sun-Sentinel, Monday, January 4, 1993

Opting out of class-action lawsuit pays off

As I have written previously, investors may opt out of a class-action suit and proceed directly against a brokerage firm through arbitration. One investor who took that course recently won an $800,000 award.

The investor, whom we'll call R.D., charged that Prudential Securities had portrayed partnerships, including Prudential Bache Energy Income, as safe and secure, comparable to certificates of deposits or municipal bonds. But in fact, he said, they were quite risky.

The attorneys who represented R.D, Michael A. Hanzman and Michael E Criden, argued that the brokerage firm failed to disclose sufficient information to enable R.D. to understand that the investment was risky.

As an example, the law firm said Prudential did not disclose that Prudential Insurance discontinued participation in the investment because of poor rates of return. Also, the law firm said Prudential borrowed money to pay out 15 percent in returns on the investment, leading investors to think that the partnerships were generating the returns.

Instead, the investors were receiving part of their own money and/or borrowed funds.

The arbitration panel's $800,000 award, included $300,000 in punitive damages.

Information on a proposed settlement has been sent to investors who bought oil and gas limited partnerships, but it was in the form of a more than 200-page book. For the average investor it was extremely difficult to understand how much money the settlement actually gave back for each unit, so it would be almost impossible for the investor to make an intelligent decision on accepting or rejecting the proposed settlement or opting out.

Also there were extremely complicated directions to fill out if an investor wanted to opt out of the class action. The investor would have to write three separate letters to three different law firms.

Because of how difficult and complicated the information was, most people would do nothing, which means they would be part of the class action and have to accept whatever dollar amount was offered.

This case shows it would be worth the time and effort to get a securities arbitration expert's opinion on whether to be part of the class action or opt out. It's your money.

Q. I have received my year-end statement from my brokerage firm. I brought it to my accountant, which I do every year so he can do my taxes. He made me aware of losses that I had no idea I had.

My broker never told me of these losses or transactions that resulted in these losses. When I called my broker and asked him to explain these trades he told me we discussed each one. That's just not true.

What recourse do I have?

A. The year-end statement from your brokerage firm is an excellent summary to review the entire year's transactions and values. It's a quick way to find out gains and losses without having to get out each buy and sell confirmation.

If you feel there were transactions that were unauthorized by you, then you would have recourse against the broker if you can prove they were unauthorized. In one case in Florida against Merrill Lynch, the claimants alleged the brokerage failed to follow trading instructions and executed unauthorized trades. Merrill Lynch denied allegation and stated claimant either authorized or ratified all trades.

Arbitrators gave the award to the claimant.

BRUCE SANKIN
Arbitration

Bruce N. Sankin, an investment counselor, is the author of What Your Stockbroker Doesn't Want You to Know. *Readers may write him at P.O. Box 77-0001, Coral Springs, Fla. 33077, or call 1-305-346-8585.*

ABUSING THE SYSTEM

Being a broker for the past 20 years, I've seen many changes in the brokerage industry. One of the major changes, in my opinion one for the better, was the acceptance of arbitration for handling disputes. No one likes problems. However, when you deal with investments that fluctuate in price, there are bound to be differences. Most brokers in the industry want to do clean business and don't want to be associated with those who don't. When I speak to other brokers they want to get the bad brokers out of the industry. You read about how bad brokers abuse clients and give the entire industry a bad reputation.

What concerns me is the following: How do you get bad clients out of the industry? There is a broker in my office who has an arbitration filing against him by a client who seems to have nothing better to do but to harass him. This client is constantly coming into the office to meet with the manager and the broker. He claims the broker should have warned him that his investment could fluctuate. The total claim is under $2,500, and he is representing himself.

After discussing this situation with a friend, who is a broker at another firm, he asked the client's name. When I told him, I found out this client had filed an arbitration with his firm under similar circumstances. That firm settled with this client because even though the broker was in the right, it was decided it would be too costly to fight the arbitration. In fact, I've noticed many firms offer to settle with a client before both the client and the firm rack up large legal expenses. In this case, it seems this client has found a way to supplement his income by filing frivolous arbitrations. I'm told once an arbitration case is filed, the brokerage firm can expect its cost to be at least a few thousand dollars. If a client is truly hurt by a bad broker and firm, then he should be compensated. But can anything be done to try to stop clients from taking advantage of the arbitration system? Are there any arbitration cases where a client had to pay for trying to abuse the system?

Usually, when you read an article about the abuses in the brokerage industry, it is about a rogue broker or firm.

It's rare, if ever, you hear about rogue clients. These are people who know how to take advantage of the system. They usually open accounts at many different brokerage firms—sometimes as many as 15 to 20 accounts around the country. They try to find the newest broker in the office with the least amount of experience. New brokers are hungry for business to prove themselves.

In the same way a client can ask for a copy of a broker's CRD to see their disciplinary history, there are databases available within the industry that keep tabs on bad customers. Your compliance people should be familiar with these. If you suspect a potential problem, give compliance a call before opening the account. If a prospect has been involved in a number of arbitrations, this could show a pattern that a broker and firm should be aware of.

There is a specific case brought to my attention where the arbitration panel not only awarded in favor of the brokerage firm and broker, but awarded monetary awards against the client in counterclaims brought by the firm and broker. In this case, the client alleged failure to execute, breach of fiduciary duty and negligence. The claimant requested damages of $28,000. The claimant tried to get the sympathy of the arbitrators by saying he was a retiree and an unsophisticated investor. What came out at the hearing was this client had more than 30 brokerage accounts. His main source of income was profits from trading securities. In 1993, he opened 18 brokerage accounts. In the next few years, he filed complaint letters with at least 10 firms accusing the brokers and firms of a number of allegations. At the hearing, he admitted to having five other arbitrations pending and to having received full payment on another claim from another brokerage firm.

The arbitrator awarded $2,500 to the brokerage firm and broker in a counterclaim for damages caused by the actions of the claimant.

Bruce Sankin is a Ft. Lauderdale, Fla.-based investment counselor who serves as an arbitrator with the NASD. He writes frequently on arbitration. Address questions for this column to: Legal Corner, Plaza Communications Inc., 18818 Teller Ave., Suite 280, Irvine, CA 92715. The author can be reached at 305/346-8585.

BY BRUCE SANKIN

BUSINESS

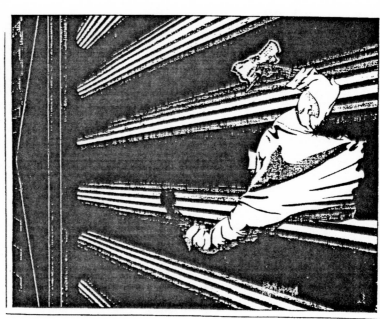

FIGHTING WALL STREET

Arbitration has taken over many investors' complaints, but who is getting the better deal, investor or brokerage? **8**

Sun illustration/JEAN WENLAUB

Pay close attention to brokerage account forms, author says.

By CHARLES LUNAN
Business Writer

Staff photo/LOU TOMAN

Financial adviser Bruce Sankin of Plantation displays a book he wrote to inform investors.

Do you own or rent your home? Do you own 10 percent or more of a business? How did you come to choose this brokerage firm to open your account?

They all seem like innocuous questions, just one more piece of paperwork in the annoying routine of opening a brokerage account. Yet investors' failure to fill out brokerage account forms themselves or their tendency to fill them out inaccurately can cost them dearly should a dispute arise with their broker, said Bruce Sankin, a broker who has recently written a book entitled *What Your Stockbroker Doesn't Want You To Know.*

"It is the only written document showing customers' profiles," said Sankin, interviewed at his home in Plantation, where he has started his own financial advisory firm after seven years working for full-service brokerage firms. "All the rest of the business done is done verbally. The only thing I can guarantee you is that if there is a dispute, your account of the conversations will be different from your broker's, so it's important to fill out the account form carefully."

Brokerages generally require a so-called account form be filled out during a customer's initial visit. The form lays out an investor's income, assets, investment objectives, occupation and prior investments.

In their eagerness to open an account, however, many investors let their brokers fill out the forms, said Maria Scott, an editor with the American Association of Individual Investors.

"People . . . are concerned about getting the account open," Scott said. "That's a different way of looking at it than from the other side of an arbitration."

Investors should insist on filling out the forms themselves and make sure they are accurate when they do. Sankin advised.

The forms are often used by brokers in arbitration hearings to justify the sale of highly speculative investments, Sankin said. One standard question that asks customers how they came to choose their broker can be particularly loaded.

"Seminars, personal acquaintances and referrals may sound innocent, but let me show you what they imply," the book says. "Brokerage firms may say if you have gone to one seminar you may have gone to many and that you are aware of different types of investments and are probably suited for many investments."

Sankin, who worked for Prudential-Bache Securities from 1987 through April, is selling the book for $29.95. For further information, write him at P.O. Box 15065, Plantation, Fla. 33318.

American Association of Individual Investors

AAII JOURNAL ®

July 1991   Volume XIII, Number 6

The Brokerage Account Form: Handle With Care

By Bruce Sankin

Stockbrokers, in general, deal honestly and with integrity with their clients. But you should always understand that they are in business to make money. The more you understand commission brokerage houses, the better value you can get for your money when dealing with them.

One aspect of dealing with brokerage houses that is often misunderstood by individual investors is the seemingly innocuous account form.

The account form is filled out either by you or your broker when you first open an account with a firm. In fact, everyone must have a completed account form to receive an account number. This is mandatory before a transaction between you and your stockbroker can occur. The account form is usually the only written document the stockbroker has that describes you.

Most investors don't give this form much thought. Yet it is an extremely important document. Why?

Let's say a dispute later arises—you feel that you were sold an investment for which you were unsuited, or about which you did not understand. If you cannot come to an amicable agreement with the brokerage firm, then arbitration could be your legal remedy. The arbitration may take place years after the original conversations between you and your stockbroker regarding the investment you purchased. Most likely, the stockbroker will remember the conversations differently than you do, thereby making the verbal discussions unreliable

Bruce Sankin is a former stockbroker and currently is an investment counselor based in Plantation, Florida. This article is excerpted from his book "What Your Stockbroker Doesn't Want You to Know" (self-published; $29.95 plus $4 shipping). It is available to AAII members for $28.00 (which includes the $4 shipping fee) from Business Publishing, P.O. Box 15065, Plantation, Florida 33318; 800/828-2536.

and meaningless. It is at this point that the account form becomes vital in your defense at arbitration. Many of the disputes that wind up in arbitration focus on the individual's investment knowledge, and the account form is one of the first documents that a brokerage firm will turn to when such a dispute occurs.

Filling Out the Form

The client account form might look like a basic questionnaire with simple questions, but it is the document that shows if you are suited for certain types of investments. Do not answer these questions lightly or inaccurately, because it could cost you in the future.

In general, the best advice is: Don't exaggerate either your experience or income on the account form. If you make $30,000 a year, do not state anything higher. When the question is about your investment experience in stocks, bonds, commodities, etc., only put the actual number of years you have been an investor. If you are trying to impress the stockbroker, don't!

Before filling out the form, you should fully understand the questions and how some of your answers may come back to haunt you if you are not careful. Thus, a review of the account form line by line is useful.

A standard client account form will contain the following questions:

1. General Information—Name, address, birthdate, Social Security number, telephone number.

So far, no problem.

2. Residence—rent or own.

If you own a home, this indicates to the brokerage firm that you are not ignorant of all types of investments. In addition, if the dispute concerns a real estate limited partnership, home ownership would indicate that you would have some idea of the liquidity and economic risks involved in real estate ownership. Thus, if the partnership had decreased in value, you would have difficulty claiming that you were unaware of the risks in real estate.

3. Legal residence if different from mailing address.

A residence other than your mailing address indicates to the brokerage firm that you may have more than one home, which is an indication of your assets.

4. Employment/Job Title/Occupation.

The type of job you hold could provide a clue to certain investment knowledge. For instance, it would tend to indicate the type of knowledge you might have pertaining to investments in certain industries.

5. Client annual income; client net worth exclusive of family residence, and estimated liquid net worth.

Do not exaggerate. Most importantly, the answer indicates what portion of your total assets is represented by the disputed investment. Having a diversified portfolio of no more than 2% to 5% of total assets in one investment may not be worth as much as in an arbitration decision as 50% in one investment.

6. Is the client on a fixed income?

If you are not drawing a regular salary but instead are relying on a fixed income, such as a pension or Social Security, as your source of yearly income, then say it. By answering yes to this question, the stockbroker should be aware that you have no additional income other than your investments, pensions, and/or Social Security, and that you will probably be a very conservative investor.

7. Is the client an officer, director or 10% stockholder in any corporation?

This tells the brokerage firm that you probably have knowledge about business and investments in general, and also that you have additional assets.

8. Citizen of U.S.A. (if other please specify).

If you are not a citizen of the U.S., there may be different tax liabilities depending on your investments and the country that you are from. The stockbroker must be aware of this for proper reporting and withholding. If you have properly informed the firm and a mistake is made, the brokerage firm, not you, could be liable for any penalties incurred.

9. Former client or account with other brokerage firm.

This shows the brokerage firm the type of investments that you may have made in the past. This will also indicate if you are knowledgeable or suited for certain types of investments.

10. Investment profile.

This is very important! If you want safety of principal and income, don't say growth! Put down only what you want. Also, do not put down that you have more investment experience in stock, bonds, options, etc., than what you actually have.

11. Introduction.

This question indicates to the brokerage firm how you chose to open an account. The options are usually seminars, walk/phone in, advertising, personal acquaintance, and referrals. Seminars, personal acquaintances, and referrals may sound innocent, but they have hidden implications. If you went to a seminar, it shows you go out of your way to get knowledge on specific investments. Brokerage firms may say if you have gone to one seminar you may have gone to others, and that you are aware of and suited for different types of investments. If you are referred to the firm by a person who is knowledgeable about investments, then there is a good chance you have had discussions about investments, which could imply that you know more about investments than what is stated on the account form.

12. References—name of bank.

If a dispute with your brokerage firm arises, references are a good source for the firm to further investigate your knowledge of investments.

13. Power of attorney.

This means someone besides yourself may have the right to handle the money in your account, as well as decide what investments should be made. Be very careful with this, since giving someone else this authority may affect your financial situation forever.

14. Account description—cash or margin.

Cash accounts are the most common. In a cash account, you buy or sell a security (stock, bond, mutual fund, etc.) and pay or receive 100% of the amount, usually within five business days. Margin accounts are used by very aggressive investors. A margin account gives you the right to borrow money on your account by using the securities in the account as collateral. For example: If you buy 100 shares of General Electric at $60 a share, the total amount you would owe is $6,000. In a margin account you could borrow up to 50% of the amount owed, which means you would pay $3,000 and the brokerage firm would lend you the other $3,000 for as long as you keep the General Electric stock in your account. Like any other loan, you will pay interest charges to the brokerage firm for as long as you owe them the $3,000. Buying on margin is very risky, and should be undertaken only after the risks are fully explained by your broker and fully understood by you.

Other Stockbroker Tidbits

It is very important to update the account form if your financial situation changes—for instance, if your spouse dies or you retire. Make sure your stockbroker is notified in writing and a new account form is filled out.

Finally, if a dispute arises between you and your broker, another fact that you should know is that the stockbroker must be licensed in the state where you are a permanent resident. If you buy securities from a stockbroker and you lose money, make sure that he was licensed in your state at the time of the transaction. If not, the trade should be voided and you should get all your money back.

"rebating" of agent commissions. The other 48 states prohibit commission breaks. American Discount Insurance (800/964-5795), says it will rebate 50 percent of commissions "on all qualifying policies."

FREE SERVICE FROM YOUR BANK

It's hardly news that banks hate to give away services. There are fees attached to just about everything your bank does for you, although there are ways of avoiding them. A few suggestions:

• If you use an ATM, don't use an "outside" credit card, which will cost you. Use your bank's own ATM network.

• The more money you have on deposit, the better the savings rate you're likely to receive. Of course, nobody is getting rich

on what banks are offering its best customers these days.

• Ask your bank to discount or waive fees on cashier's or traveler's checks.

• Keep an eye on the balance requirements of checking and savings accounts. Maintain minimum balances to avoid fees.

SAVING ON STOCKBROKERS

Most people pay far too much money to use the services and limited financial advice offered by brokers. For starters, since brokers stand to make a commission from everything they recommend, their advice may not be in your best interest. So it pays to shop around for financial advice and products. We asked Bruce Sankin, author of *What Your Stockbroker Doesn't Want You to*

Know (Business Publishing, Coral Springs, Fla., 305/346-8585), for his advice on reducing brokerage costs:

• Do your research and shop for "no-load" (no sales charge) mutual funds. See the March/April issue of CD for details.

• Tell your broker to send you an old copy of the Standard and Poor's book of stock listings, which lists stocks, price histories, dividend yields and other financial information. Most brokers throw out their old copies. An S&P subscription would cost you $150.

• If you invest in mutual funds through a broker, ask for a fund in a large "family" of funds. That way, if your objectives change, you can switch into another fund without paying new sales charges.

• Avoid any broker-sold funds that charge a fee for reinvesting dividends.

• Avoid any "proprietary" investments that brokers sell at initial offering; the returns may not benefit you as much as it benefits them.

• Remember that a margin account is actually a loan against the securities you have in your account. Although it allows you to purchase more securities, you can lose more than you intend.

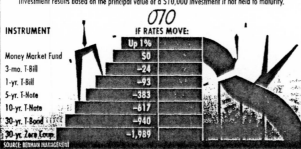

HOW INTEREST RATES MOVE

Investment results based on the principal value of a $10,000 investment if not held to maturity.

INSTRUMENT	IF RATES MOVE:
	Up 1%
Money Market Fund	$0
3-mo. T-Bill	-24
1-yr. T-Bill	-93
5-yr. T-Note	-383
10-yr. T-Note	-617
30-yr. T-Bond	-940
30-yr. Zero Coup.	-1,989

SOURCE: BENHAM MANAGEMENT

FUNDS VS. BONDS: HOW TO PLAY IT SAFE

Who could have predicted that interest rates would fall so consistently that some of the best investments would be bonds? But hold onto your hats. The investments that appear to be the most conservative may turn out to be the riskiest. You make money in trading long-term bonds only if interest rates fall, so you're taking a big risk if they rise.

Here's basically how bond prices work: the longer the maturity, the more risk you take. In this case, your safest bet is that boring $1-a-share money-market fund that doesn't lose principal. Since bond prices are pegged to the rate of inflation, they do well in times of low inflation and stability. When inflation roars back, investors don't want to be stuck with yesterday's paltry bond rates, so they dump the old stuff for higher yields.

If you believe we will see slow economic growth or a lingering recession, then your best (but riskiest) investment is a 30-year Zero Coupon Bond (or mutual fund that holds such vehicles). With this investment, you can gain $2,665 on an investment of $10,000 if rates fall 1 percent. If they *rise* 1 percent, however, you lose $1,989. On the safe end, if rates rise—and you invest in a money-market fund—you gain from the higher yields and lose no principal. Taking marginally more risk, you'll lose only $24 on a $10,000 U.S. Treasury bill if rates jump 1 percent (see the table above).

Is playing the interest-rate game an "all or nothing" proposition? It doesn't have to be if you diversify across maturities, bond types (government and corporate) and even some high-yielding utilities stocks.

IRS DEBUNKS TAX MYTHS

You can believe whatever you like, but everybody's favorite federal agency is out to debunk a few myths. For example, some accountants have long claimed that the earlier you file, the greater chance you have of getting audited. The IRS counters that it uses a computer program that runs throughout the year to "flag" returns for auditing.

Does attaching the preprinted name and address label conceal a special code for audit selection, as some bean counters believe? The IRS insists that the label only serves to "reduce the chance for error and cuts the processing cost." Some even think that calling the IRS tax-assistance lines boosts one's chances of being audited. Not so, the agency retorts. IRS employees never ask for names or Social Security numbers "unless they're needed to resolve a tax-account matter."

No matter what the IRS claims, Americans could use better tax advice. Tax refunds are averaging $1,140, up 1.6 percent over last year. This means more people are overestimating what they owe the government—and giving it an interest-free loan for at least 16 months. When was the last time the government did that for you?

REVERSE MORTGAGES PROVIDE CASH

For many retired and elderly people, their homes are their largest single asset. However, too many become "house rich but hoped-to-be-savior "Inaki" Lopez to Volkswagen, a move that ultimately led to charges of industrial espionage by GM. Keller also considers the broader issue of how globalization affects highly institutionalized national industries and implies that the struggle among General Motors, Toyota, and Volkswagen is symbolic of a greater cultural battle among America, Japan, and Germany.—*David Rouse*

Lamont, Edward M. The Ambassador from Wall Street: The Story of Thomas W. Lamont, J. P. Morgan's Chief Executive. Nov. 1993. 523p. index. Madison, $26.95 (1-56833-018-9). Galley.
332.1092 [B] Lamont, Thomas W. ‖ Bankers—U.S.—Biography [BKL]

There are a number of individuals who have played a significant role in shaping the U.S., yet whose names are unfamiliar to most Americans. Such a person was J. P. Morgan's CEO Thomas W. Lamont, a man who advised U.S. presidents and other world leaders and helped set economic and financial policy between the two world wars. Lamont's role has been acknowledged in scholarly and specialized histories, such as Warren I. Cohen's *Chinese Connection* (1978), which focuses on Lamont's influence on early U.S.-Chinese and U.S.-Japanese relations. There has never been, however, a biographical profile of Lamont. His grandson Edward, himself active in international banking for nearly a quarter of a century, here offers a thorough portrait based on previously unreleased and extensive personal and family correspondence that the elder Lamont left behind. Not only do we get a firsthand look at history in the making, but we also get glimpses of major social and cultural personalities, such as Charles Lindberg and H. G. Wells. Recommended for banking, foreign affairs, and history collections. —*David Rouse*

Leonhardt, Mary. Parents Who Love Reading, Kids Who Don't: How It Happens and What You Can Do about It. 1993. 256p. index. Crown, $20 (0-517-59164-2). Galley.
372.41 Reading—U.S.—Parent participation ‖ Children—U.S.—Books and reading ‖ Education—U.S.—Parent participation [CIP] 93-16655

Focusing on reading rather than on books per se, Leonhardt, a veteran English teacher, lays most of the blame for the "endemic dislike" of reading among today's kids on the doorstep of the educational establishment. She doesn't, however, let parents off scot-free; she's convinced that if anything can be done to rekindle kids' interest, it must be done at home. But literary purists beware. Comic books, magazines, series books, and various forms of subliterature are an integral part of her plan to reclaim kids lost to TV, video games, and after-school jobs. In very practical terms, she explains how parents can mix these materials with books that have enduring appeal for young people and how they can help their reluctant school-age readers handle problems that arise in class. Parents may bristle at Leonhardt's displeasure with tracking, her doubts about special education services, and the drastic measures she suggests to curb the TV habit, but they'll still recognize her commitment to kids and to reading. Although she includes tips for teaching reading to the very young and reading suggestions for children as young as eight or nine, she seems more comfortable and conversant with materials for young people junior high age and up. —*Stephanie Zvirin*

Mayer, Musa. Examining Myself: One Woman's Story of Breast Cancer Treatment and Recovery. Oct. 1993. 172p. Faber, $19.95 (0-571-19828-7). Galley.
362.19699449 [B] Mayer, Musa—Health ‖ Breast—Cancer—Patients—Biography [OCLC] 93-21598

Mayer quietly tells her story of failure to diagnose breast cancer despite mammograms and of what she found out about the medical profession, support groups, and herself. Hers is not the usual brash or flip presentation designed for the Sunday supplements or TV. When she finally was diagnosed, Mayer sought information first from reading and then from support groups. A major argument with her surgeons (which, to her later regret, she lost) arose when she wanted to have a mastectomy and reconstructive work done in close sequence. Details of her own and others' responses to surgery and chemotherapy underline the variation in individual reactions. Also individual is her decision, after experiencing leaks and other problems and despite her surgeon's objections, to have her original implant removed. She concludes with brief descriptions of new methods of treatment. Mayer raises many stimulating questions, and her low-key story deserves wide consideration. —*William Beatty*

Newton, Michael. Bad Girls Do It! An Encyclopedia of Female Murderers. Nov. 1993. 208p. Loompanics Unlimited, paper, $14.95 (1-55950-104-9). Galley.
364.1523 Women murderers ‖ Mass murder ‖ Serial murders [BKL]
Newton, Michael. Raising Hell: An Encyclopedia of Devil Worship and Satanic Crime. 1993. 406p. illus. Avon, paper, $5.99 (0-380-76837-2).

What are bad girls like these doing in a nice place like Booklist?

133.422 Satanism ‖ Cults ‖ Occultism ‖ Violent crimes [BKL] 93-90233

He's ba-ack! Who's *he*? you ask. The maven of murder and mayhem, Michael Newton, that's who. His original biographical dictionary of heinous offenders, *Hunting Humans* (1990), is sort of back, too, in hunks that fit the scopes of these two new references. For instance, humanhunters David Berkowitz (the Son of Sam killer) and Charles Manson both get carried over into *Raising Hell* because of their associations with the Four P Movement, a satanic cult that likes to kill dogs and drink their blood. Some of the *Bad Girls* are also repeaters from the earlier opus, which, with its concentration on serial killers, overlaps *Bad Girls'* focus upon female multiple murderers. Yet there are lots of new entries in *Bad Girls*, too—enough to make it seem that Newton wasn't looking hard for lady killers (as opposed to ladykillers, like Ted Bundy) back when. And there is much new material in *Raising Hell* as well, for in it Newton includes nonpersonal subjects ("Animal Sacrifice," "Child Abuse," "Heavy Metal Music," etc.), one-time homicides, and nonmurderous criminals as long as they intersect satanism. In

---

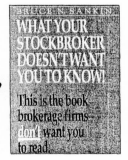

Booklist recommends*

WHAT YOUR STOCKBROKER DOESN'T WANT YOU TO KNOW by Bruce Sankin. May 1993. 181p. Business Publishing Inc., P.O. Box 77-0001, Coral Springs, FL 33077; distributed by Baker & Taylor. $20 (0-9629811-1-7).

"[Sankin] has it pretty well honed. . . . He makes the case that investors need to be highly aggressive consumers when buying and selling securities through a brockerage firm, offering specific money-saving tips and suggestions based on his inside knowledge of how brokers operate. However, it's . . . how Sankin details the arbitration process of the National Association of Security Dealers that make this book unique. . . . Of more than 4,000 cases in 1991, Sankin says that investors recovered at least part of thier money 75 percent of the time.

LIBRARIES . . . SHOULD CONSIDER AT LEAST ONE REFERENCE COPY OF THIS EYE-OPENER." *David Rouse. *Booklist*, April 1, 1993

LONG ISLAND UNIVERSITY

September 27, 1991

To: Bruce Sankin

From: Dr. Christopher L. Hayes
       National Center for Women and Retirement Research

Subject: Book Endorsement

It is with great pleasure that the National Center for
Women and Retirement Research endorses your recent book. This
publication will be of tremendous benefit to the thousands of
individuals who find themselves the victims of investment
fraud and unprofessional investment practices. Of special value
is how you articulate a step-by-step process to utilize the
arbitration process to recoup monies lost.

As you are aware, a major mission of the National Center is
to make women aware of the importance of being informed
financial consumers. Your book will be recommended reading
for women who attend our financial seminars. Again, we applaud
this most important work.

EMANUEL M. KRAKAUER
ATTORNEY AT LAW
THE MONADNOCK BUILDING
53 WEST JACKSON BOULEVARD, SUITE 1440
CHICAGO, ILLINOIS 60604
TELEPHONE (312) 362-1100 · FAX (312) 362-1234

November 24, 1992

Mr. Bruce N. Sankin
P.O. Box 77-0001
Coral Springs, Florida 33077

Dear Mr. Sankin,

I just wanted to thank you again for all your help. You may recall that I called you as a stranger out of the blue some two weeks ago seeking advice concerning an investment of my parents after my mother told me of her problem and enclosed copies of your column.

When my mother and father purchased two funds with my father's retirement income, they were told in no uncertain terms that their principal of $200,000 was guaranteed, and without a doubt they would not have placed their retirement monies into the funds but for that unequivocal assurance. Now, some six years later my surviving mother has come to learn for that far from the principal she has continually since then been induced to believe to be untouched and untouchable, her funds in reality were in a limited partnership with her current principal value reduced by approximately $123,000.00.

With the invaluable aid of your generous time, advice, direction, and assistance throughout our following phone conversations I have been above to secure a settlement with the firm in question in a manner that makes my mother virtually whole. I can't begin to fully express in words how much you have done to reverse what had seemed to be the brink of an emotional and financial nightmare into a gratifying resolution.

If I can ever be of any service to you in anyway, please do not hesitate to call upon me.

With warmest personal thanks I am

Sincerely,

Emanuel M. Krakauer

337 N. E. 2 Court
Dania, Florida 33004
October 6, 1992

Mr. Bruce Sankin
P. O. Box 77-0001
Coral Springs, Florida 33077

Dear Mr. Sankin:

I would like to thank you for your excellent Sun-Sentinel newspaper
articles dealing with arbitration by the NASD. Quite a few of the
cases you wrote about paralleled an experience I had a few years ago.
It was through your column in the newspaper that I learned that
there was such an avenue as arbitration of a claim against a
brokerage firm and one of its brokers.

My case is now in arbitration. Whether I win or lose, I still
thank you for making me aware of the fact that I did have recourse.
When my case is settled, I will be happy to supply you with
another interesting arbitration example for your readers.

Keep up the good work.

Sincerely,

Robert J. Bakus

Louis D. Sill
3300 NE 191 St
Apt 1217
Aventura, Fl 33180

7/29/92

Mr. Bruce Sankin
P. O. Box 77-0001
Coral Springs, Fl 33077

Dear Mr. Sankin,

I have recently purchased a copy of your book "WHAT YOUR STOCKBROKER DOESN'T WANT YOU TO KNOW" and I wish to register a complaint.

Let me clarify the particulars of my complaint:

1. I needed this book in September of 1986 when I placed a sizable investment in the market. Almost all of it unsuitable for my particular needs.

2. Had you written this book in a more timely manner I would have been a much better position to purchase investments more suited to my needs and not as likely to have lost over $65,000 in poorly performing funds.

HOWEVER: Please note....Because of information that I found in your book once I did read it encouraged me to file for arbitration and listed the steps I must take to take such action!! I am most hopeful that armed with this knowledge I will have a hedge to challenge a huge concern.

Sincerely

Louis D. Sill

P.S. You are welcome to use this testimonial in any maner you see fit.

LAURA A. PARK

**1898 Lago Vista Boulevard
Palm Harbor, FL 34685**

October 10, 1995

Mr. Bruce Sankin
1749 N.W. 88th Way
Coral Springs, FL 33071

**RE: LAURA A. PARK VS.
FIRST UNION BROKERAGE SERVICES, INC.**

Dear Bruce:

Thank you so much for your help in my arbitration proceeding against First Union.

I believe that your role as an expert witness was an important factor in the positive outcome of my case. All of your knowledge and experience in the brokerage industry, combined with your sincere concern about the injustice rendered to me, had a tremendous impact on the favorable verdict.

Thank you again for your help.

Sincerely yours,

Laura A. Park

Laura A. Park